GCSE Learning for Life and Work for CCEA

Amanda McAleer

David McVeigh

Michaella O'Boyle

Editor: Brigid McStravick

HODDER
EDUCATION
AN HACHETTE UK COMPANY

The Publishers would like to thank the following for permission to reproduce copyright material:

Photo credits
p. 7 *tl* © JoeFox/Alamy, *tc* Mike Hewitt/Getty Images, *tr* Rex Features, *bl* Rex Features, *bc* Elizabeth Leyden/Alamy, *br* © JoeFox/Alamy; **p. 9** © Roger Bradley/Alamy; **p. 11** Niall Carson/PA Wire/Press Association Images; **p. 15** LIU KAI/LANDOV/Press Association Images; **p. 18** Keystone/Getty Images; **p. 19** Nickelsberg/Time Life Pictures/Getty Images; **p. 22** © Tim Graham/Alamy; **p. 25** *l & r* Equality Commission for N Ireland (www.equalityni.org); **p. 27** Jim Young, Pool/AP Photo/PA Photos; **p. 28** *tl* Paul Faith/PA Archive/PA Photos, *tr* © Libby Welch/Alamy, *bl* DUP/Getty Images, *br* © Mark Gwilliam/Alamy; **p. 29** *l* Peter Macdiarmid/Getty Images, *r* © Nick Cobbing/Greenpeace; **p. 31** *tl* © Jon Le-Bon – Fotolia.com, *tr* Anupam Nath/AP Photo/PA Photos, *bl* Muhammed Muheisen/AP Photo/PA Photos, *br* ABDURASHID ABIKAR/AFP/Getty Images; **p. 33** Andy Eames/AP Photo/PA Photos; **p. 34** Hugh O'Neill – Fotolia; **p. 35** © Jiri Kabele/iStockphoto.com; **p. 37** GK Hart/Vikki Hart/Getty Images; **p. 40** ©Photodisc/Getty Images; **p. 42** © iofoto – Fotolia.com; **p. 47** John Birdsall/Press Association Images; **p. 48** © Kent Knudson/PhotoLink/Photodisc/Getty Images; **p. 49** Afton Almaraz/AP Photo/PA Photos; **p. 50** Anthony Devlin/PA Wire/Press Association Images; **p. 51** Chris Young/PA Archive/Press Association Images; **p. 52** © Josemaria Toscano – Fotolia; **p. 58** © WHO 2010; **p. 60** *t* © Pavel Losevsky – Fotolia.com, *b* © Friday – Fotolia; **p. 63** Mental Health Foundation; **p. 65** *l* © Crown copyright 2011/http://www.nhs.uk/Change4Life, *r* DAVID BOILY/AFP/Getty Images; **p. 66** Crown Copyright; **p. 67** Johnny Green/PA Wire/Press Association Images; **p. 68** *t* © SimpleVision – Fotolia, *b* © Stockbyte/Getty Images; **p. 71** © Bubbles Photolibrary/Alamy; **p. 74** *tr* © istockphoto.com/ Alan Crawford, *cl* © Imagestate Media, *cr* © Krasser – Fotolia.com, *bl* © omer sukru goksu/iStockphoto.com, *br* © Imagestate Media; **p. 75** *t* © Bubbles Photolibrary/Alamy, *c* © Imagestate Media, *b* © silencefoto – Fotolia.com; **p. 76** *l* © Jana Lumley – Fotolia.com, *r* © Scott Griessel – Fotolia; **p. 77** *t* © Imagestate Media, *b* © Gina Sanders – Fotolia; **p. 78** © JLP/Jose L. Pelaez/Corbis; **p. 79** ©Crown Copyright/Courtesy of Press Association Images; **p. 81** Christopher Dodge – Fotolia; **p. 86** © Design Pics Inc./Alamy; **p. 91** *t* .shock – Fotolia, *b* Vladimir Wrangel – Fotolia; **p. 92** *t* © 2010 Twitter , *cr* © 2010 Microsoft, *cl* © 2010 Last.fm Ltd; *b* ©2003-2010 Myspace inc.; **p. 94** Most Wanted/Rex Features; **p. 95** *t* © Imagestate Media, *b* © Imagestate Media; **p. 99** © Juriah Mosin – Fotolia; **p. 101** Leticia Wilson – Fotolia; **p. 102** ©Photodisc/Getty Images; **p. 103** Daniel Acker/Bloomberg via Getty Images; **105** ©Photodisc/Getty Images; **p. 108** © Kevin Eaves – Fotolia; **p. 112** © FoodIgredients/Alamy; **p. 113** © Markos Dolopikos/Alamy; **p. 116** *tl* © gerenme/iStockphoto.com, *tr* ©Photodisc/Getty Images, *bl* © Stockbyte/Getty Images, *br* © Imagestate Media; **p. 118** HaywireMedia – Fotolia; **p. 124** *t* © Photodisc/Getty Images, *c* © simon denson/Alamy, *b* Balkis Press/ABACAPRESS.COM; **p. 126** *t* © Vasily Smirnov – Fotolia, *bl* Steve Vidler/ Imagestate RM/Photolibrary Group, *br* ©Photodisc/Getty Images; **p. 127** © Steven Vona – Fotolia; **p. 131** *l* © Misha – Fotolia.com, *r* © ManicBlu – Fotolia.com; **p. 135** *tl* © Imagestate Media, *tr* © makuba – Fotolia.com, *bl* ©Photodisc/Getty Images, *br* Frederic Sierakowski/Rex Features; **p.137** screenshots: *tl* with thanks to Careers Service NI, *tr* with thanks to Job Centre, *b* with thanks to EGSA (Educational Guidance Service for Adults) **p. 147** *t* © Design Pics Inc./Alamy, *b* © pressmaster – Fotolia.com; **p. 151** © David H. Lewis/istockphoto.com; **p. 158** *l* © David Robertson/Alamy, *tr* © David Cordner Main 3/Alamy, *cr* © David Cordner Main 4/Alamy, *br* © Richard Wayman/Alamy; *tl* © scenicireland.com/Christopher Hill Photographic/Alamy, *cl* © David Cordner Main 2/Alamy, *bl* © Caroline Jones/Alamy, *r* © Stephen Barnes/Northern Ireland/Alamy; **p. 161** Yui Mok/PA Archive/Press Association Images; **p. 162** ©2010 Innocent; **p. 164** *l* ©Photodisc/Getty Images, *r* © Klaus Tiedge/istockphoto.com; **p. 168** © michele Galli/iStockphoto.com.

Acknowledgements
p.8: 'Take a closer look' brochure, website extract, adapted from *www.nitakeacloserlook.com*; **p.12** Vicious Circle of Prejudice diagram based on an idea by PlayBoard; **pp. 14, 24, 36, 71,125:** extracts from articles from *Belfast Telegraph*; **pp.48–49:** Friends of the Earth, Case study, text from *http://www.foe.co.uk/ campaigns/biodiversity/issues/saving_forests_18269.html*; **p.56:** Northern Ireland Human Rights Commission, website extract from *www.nihrc.org*; **p.80:** Debatewise, Online article about alcohol from *http://debatewise.org/debates/589-should-cheap-alcohol-be-banned*; **p.89:** BBC, 'Slink – Sex, Love and Life – A to Z of You – Peer Pressure', extract from *www.bbc.co.uk/switch/slink/sexlovelife/index.shtml?index.shtml?page=life&sub=peer*; **p.92:** Table: Age profile of UK social networking site category visitors, May 2009 from *comScore World metrix*; **p.118:** Biznet IIS, Case study from *www.biznetiis.com*; **p.156:** Tricia Holly Davies, 'Weather-related problems have been underestimated by scientists', adapted from *Times Online* (22 March 2009), © 2009 News International; **p.161:** BBC, Web article on Duncan Bannatyne, adapted from *http://www.bbc.co.uk/dragonsden/dragons/duncanbannatyne.shtml*; **pp.168–** Case study: Debbie Chestnutt and her Monkey Business from *www.nibusinessinfo.co.uk*, © Crown copyright.

Crown copyright material is reproduced under Class Licence Number C02P0000060 with the permission of the Controller of HMSO.

Every effort has been made to trace all copyright holders, but if any have been inadvertently overlooked the Publishers will be pleased to make the necessary arrangements at the first opportunity.

Although every effort has been made to ensure that website addresses are correct at time of going to press, Hodder Education cannot be held responsible for the content of any website mentioned in this book. It is sometimes possible to find a relocated web page by typing in the address of the home page for a website in the URL window of your browser.

Hachette UK's policy is to use papers that are natural, renewable and recyclable products and made from wood grown in sustainable forests. The logging and manufacturing processes are expected to conform to the environmental regulations of the country of origin.

Orders: please contact Bookpoint Ltd, 130 Milton Park, Abingdon, Oxon OX14 4SB. Telephone: (44) 01235 827720. Fax: (44) 01235 400454. Lines are open 9.00–5.00, Monday to Saturday, with a 24-hour message answering service. Visit our website at www.hoddereducation.co.uk

© David McVeigh, Amanda McAleer, Michaella O'Boyle 2011
First published in 2011 by
Hodder Education,
An Hachette UK Company
338 Euston Road
London NW1 3BH

Impression number   5 4
Year   2015 2014 2013

Cover photo © Paul Vismara/Stock Illustration Source /Getty Images
Illustrations by Oxford Designers and Illustrators
Typeset in Formata Light 10.5 pt/14pt by DC Graphic Design Limited, Swanley, Kent
Printed in Dubai

A catalogue record for this title is available from the British Library

ISBN: 9781444120752

Contents

Introduction

About the book

This book has been written to support the CCEA GCSE Learning for Life and Work specification.

The book is divided into three areas of study, following the order and content requirements of the specification. These are:

- Local and Global Citizenship
- Personal Development
- Employability

Each of the three areas of study in the book is divided into sections. Each section:

- starts with the learning outcomes from the specification, which outline what you should learn from studying that part of the course
- contains a variety of activities which, depending on the type of activity, can be carried out individually, in pairs or in groups. These will help you to understand and explore relevant issues as well as developing independent thinking and decision-making skills
- lists the key words you should know the meaning of; these are defined in the glossary at the end of the book.

About the course

During this course you have to study the three areas of study outlined above. These provide a comprehensive, worthwhile course of study and contribute to developing you as a young person and a participant in society. The content and activities throughout the book build on the skills and knowledge you developed in Key Stage 3. The activities give you the opportunity to develop further your skills of managing information, problem-solving and decision-making, being creative, working with others and self-management. Studying this course will help you to understand current events

and provide a basis for your future as an active citizen in society. At the end of the course you should have the ability to explore the challenges and opportunities that personal, social, cultural, economic and political issues pose in everyday society.

The course also develops your skills to think independently and make informed decisions in relation to personal, social, economic and employment issues. You will also have the opportunity to think critically about various issues and to understand the relevance of the course in relation to your own experiences and aspirations.

The examination

For each of the areas of study you will have to complete a written examination paper. These can either be taken altogether at the end of the course in a terminal examination or individually throughout the course as modular examinations.

For each area of study the modular paper is divided into two sections (A and B):

Section A

There are three questions in Section A (Questions 1–3) and all questions must be answered. The questions allow you to demonstrate and apply your knowledge and understanding of the particular area of study. Each question states what area of the content the question is from. For example:

This question is about issues of self-employment and sources of support.

Each of the three questions is further divided into three parts. In order to achieve the maximum 20 marks you need to be aware of what is expected for each type of question:

Question 1(a)

This part of the question is worth one mark and will begin with the phrase, 'Complete the following sentence' or the word 'Name'. For example:

1(a) Name the term for the group that looks after employees' rights.

Your answer should simply state the answer. For example:

> *Trade Union.*

Question 1(b) and 1(c)

These parts of Question 1 are worth two marks each and will ask you to 'Identify and explain' something. For example:

1(b) Identify **and** explain **one** way in which a young person's health and well-being can be supported by their school.

Four lines will be provided in the examination paper for you to answer this question. It is important that you identify **one** way and then explain it. For example:

> *Pastoral care from teachers because teachers are trained to listen and advise students facing emotional or physical health problems.*

One mark will be given for the identification (e.g. 'Pastoral care from teachers') and one mark for the explanation (e.g. 'because teachers are trained …'). If you identify two separate ways with no explanation of either of them then you can only get one mark. In your explanation you should use the words 'because' or 'and so'.

Question 2(a)

This part of the question is worth one mark and takes the same format as Question 1(a).

Question 2(b) and 2(c)

These parts of Question 2 are worth two marks each and will ask you to 'Explain' something. For example:

2(b) Explain **one** danger of alcohol to a young person's health.

Four lines will be provided in the examination paper for you to answer this question. It is important that you explain **one** danger and do not write down two dangers with no explanation. For example:

> *Alcohol is dangerous because it can cause liver damage which can result in alcoholic poisoning through cirrhosis of the liver.*

In your explanation you need to answer the question. For example, for the question above you would need to show the examiner that you understand the dangers of alcohol. In your explanation you should use the words 'because' or 'and so'.

Question 3(a)

This part of the question is worth two individual marks and takes the same format as Question 1(a) and 2(a) except that it will ask you to name two things. For example:

3(a) Name **two** ways a person can express their cultural identity.

In your answer you simply need to write down two ways. For example:

> *Music and language.*

Question 3(b) and 3(c)

These parts of Question 3 are identical to Question 1(b) and 1(c) and are worth two marks each. You will be asked to 'Identify and explain' something.

Section B

There are two questions in Section B (Questions 4 and 5) and both questions must be answered. There is a maximum of 20 marks available for this section and quality of written communication will be assessed in your answers. This means your style of writing, spelling, grammar and punctuation will be taken into account when answering both these questions.

A piece of information called **Source A** is provided to help you answer both Questions 4 and 5 along with your own knowledge.

SOURCE A

The Growth of New Technologies

Northern Ireland faces changing employment patterns as a result of the growth of new technologies.

Over the past number of years, technology has changed dramatically and this affects the type of jobs and skills that are required in the workplace.

Improved technology has meant that many manual jobs have been replaced by automated processes. As a result of this, many workers have had to retrain and learn new skills.

The Internet has enabled businesses to trade in the global market. They buy and sell goods and services all over the world using the Internet.

Question 4(a)

In this part of the question you are asked to explain two reasons/ways or provide an explanation of two terms. Each of these reasons/ways will be awarded two marks each. For example:

4(a) Read **Source A** and use it to help you answer this question.

Explain what is meant by:
(i) 'retrain'
(ii) 'the global market'.

In your answer you have to explain both terms.
For example:

> **(i)** Attend a training course in order to learn new skills.
>
> **(ii)** Having access to a worldwide market in order to buy and sell goods and services all over the world.

Question 4(b)

In this part of the question you are asked to explain something using the source provided to help you answer. For example:

4(b) Read **Source A** and use it to help you answer this question.

Explain how technology has resulted in changes in employment patterns over the past number of years.

A maximum of six marks can be awarded for this answer and it is marked in levels. In order to achieve the highest level (Level 3) you need to identify most of the points made in the source and provide a detailed, clear explanation using specialist vocabulary. For example:

> Advances in technology over the past number of years have meant that employment patterns are now focused around computerisation and as a result of this more jobs are based on computer skills. Nowadays skills taught to students in school are of a technological nature at the expense of traditional skills and therefore traditional skills are diminishing in the workplace. Employees still working in traditional industries are now forced to retrain and learn new skills as a result of job losses caused by cheaper labour, cheap imports and modern technology.

Question 5

In this question you are asked to evaluate something with reference to the source provided. For example:

5 With reference to **Source A and** your own knowledge evaluate the impact on a business of trading on the Internet.

The word **'evaluate'** is the key word in this question. This means you need to explain 'positives' and 'negatives' when writing your answer. A maximum of ten marks can be awarded for this answer and it is marked in levels. In order to achieve the highest level (Level 3) you must provide a detailed analysis and focus on both positive and negative factors. Do not just write down a list of positives and negatives. Your answer needs to be written in paragraphs and needs to flow from one paragraph to the next. For example:

Trading on the Internet means that a business is open 24 hours a day, seven days a week and this should lead to an increase in sales. With this increase in sales, the business will obviously increase its profits. As a result of trading on the Internet, businesses will undoubtedly save money as they may not have to pay out as much money on showrooms and premises from which to sell their products.

Advertising costs can be kept to a minimum as the business will not have to ensure that their products are advertised using an advertising campaign. The business could become better known all over the world owing to their sales across the global market.

However it must be noted that there is also a negative aspect of trading on the Internet.

Having a worldwide market will mean that the business will face a lot of competition and on account of this the business will have to ensure that it carries out a lot of market research in a comprehensive manner in order to assess the requirements of customers in such a wide market.

Designing and updating a website may prove expensive for a business as specialists may need to be employed in order to carry this out on a regular basis so that customers are kept informed of all the latest developments.

Obviously the business will have to be aware of the costs of packaging and distribution to customers all over the world as this may prove to be a very expensive cost to the business.

Section 1 Diversity and inclusion in Northern Ireland and the wider world

Learning outcomes

I am learning about:

* the ways in which people in Northern Ireland express their different cultural identities
* the positive contribution of different ethnic groups to Northern Ireland's society
* conflict and its resolution without recourse to violence
* strategies for promoting a more inclusive society.

This first section looks at the changing social landscape of Northern Ireland, and how people in Northern Ireland express their different cultural identities. It explores the positive contribution made by ethnic minorities to Northern Ireland's society. It also examines how conflicts of identity can arise and explores strategies for promoting a more inclusive and cohesive society. Finally, it investigates how we can embrace and promote cultural diversity in school, the community and the workplace.

Expressing our cultural identity

Our identity is formed by our personal experiences, our background and other factors such as the homes we live in, the community we belong to and the school we attend. There are various aspects to our identity such as age, gender, ethnic origin and religious beliefs. Identity is about who we are and who we would like to be. We can choose some aspects of our identity although many aspects cannot be changed.

Although we are all different, we do share many things in common and, in society, most people belong to a social or cultural group and have a particular cultural identity. Our cultural identity is formed by the language, beliefs, traditions and customs of the society we come from. In Northern Ireland, our cultural identity is usually linked to our religious/political background and what nationality we consider ourselves to be.

Over the last few years Northern Ireland has become a more culturally **diverse** society. With an increase in the number of people from other countries choosing to

live here, Northern Ireland can no longer be viewed as a **bi-cultural** country, consisting of simply two cultures (Unionist and Nationalist); it is, instead, a **multicultural** country.

However, despite these changes, it is important to recognise that there are still two main cultural identities in Northern Ireland; these are widely recognised as Protestant/**Unionist**, and Catholic/**Nationalist**.

In Northern Ireland people express their cultural identity in many ways; for example, through:

* food and drink
* music
* festivals and parades
* sport
* language
* clothes/dress
* religious and political beliefs
* flags, emblems and murals

▲ This collage shows how the two main cultural groups in Northern Ireland express their cultural identity.

Activity

1. Carry out the activity below in pairs.

   a) Using the Internet as well as the information and images on pages 6–7 and your own knowledge, compare some of the ways the two main traditions in Northern Ireland express their cultural identity by completing the table below. Some of the boxes can have more than one example.

   b) Using the information from the table, outline **two** differences and **two** similarities between these two groups.

   c) Discuss your results with another pair and present your findings to the rest of the class.

	Music	Festivals	Flags/symbols	Sport	Language	Food and drink
Nationalist				Gaelic football		
Unionist		Orange Order parades				

Key words

bi-cultural ■ diversity ■ multicultural ■ Nationalist ■ Unionist

Ethnic minorities in Northern Ireland

Living in a society with different cultures can bring many benefits and opportunities, including mutual understanding through learning about each other's cultures.

This can help break down barriers, build trust and ultimately promote respect within society as people share their different cultural experiences and beliefs with one another.

Today there are many different ethnic groups living in Northern Ireland; many were born here, others have chosen to make Northern Ireland their home. For example, the 2009 school census recorded that in schools across Northern Ireland there were 7000 newcomer children speaking 40 different languages.

Activity

1. Using Source A and your own knowledge, answer the following questions.

   a) Identify and explain **one** way in which Northern Ireland is changing.

   b) Explain what is meant by a 'multicultural' and 'bi-cultural society'.

   c) Identify and explain **two** ways in which cultural diversity can enrich society in Northern Ireland.

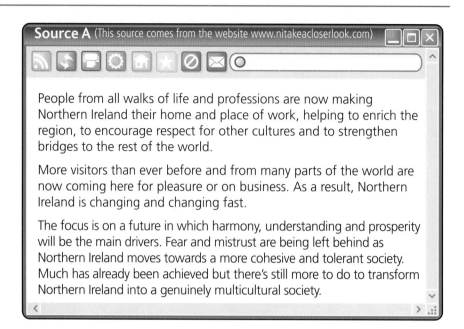

Source A (This source comes from the website www.nitakeacloserlook.com)

People from all walks of life and professions are now making Northern Ireland their home and place of work, helping to enrich the region, to encourage respect for other cultures and to strengthen bridges to the rest of the world.

More visitors than ever before and from many parts of the world are now coming here for pleasure or on business. As a result, Northern Ireland is changing and changing fast.

The focus is on a future in which harmony, understanding and prosperity will be the main drivers. Fear and mistrust are being left behind as Northern Ireland moves towards a more cohesive and tolerant society. Much has already been achieved but there's still more to do to transform Northern Ireland into a genuinely multicultural society.

Cultural influences

Imagine how dull life would be if we all looked alike, thought alike and acted alike! Northern Ireland's society is enriched by the wide variety of food, language, sport and music that having an ethnically diverse society brings. One example is the range of different sports that are played in Northern Ireland, such as Australian rules football, baseball, basketball, Gaelic football, hurling, ice hockey, netball, rugby and many more.

Other examples of Northern Ireland's ethnic diversity can be seen through the variety of cultural events celebrated across the region. These newspaper headlines from the *Belfast Telegraph* in 2009 give a snapshot of some of these.

School embraces world culture on Language Day

Jewish culture is celebrated in north Belfast

Botanic to unveil Chinese mural

Activities

2. Choose one of the ethnic groups listed below and carry out research, using the Internet or newspapers, to find examples of how they celebrate their culture in Northern Ireland.

    Chinese ▪ Indian ▪ Polish ▪ African ▪ Jewish

3. In groups of four, discuss how you could celebrate cultural diversity within (a) your school; and (b) your local community. Each group should appoint a scribe, a chairperson, a spokesperson and a timekeeper. The spokesperson should then present your findings to the rest of the class.

◄ This photograph shows public art on display in Victoria Square, Belfast.

Economic influences

People coming to Northern Ireland from other countries contribute to the economy through bringing skills and labour to areas where there is a shortage (see pages 120–123 for more information on this).

In the health sector, for example, workers from India and the Philippines are employed as doctors, nurses, and carers, providing essential support and care to the aged, ill and those who are most vulnerable.

In the private sector there are many **immigrants** from different ethnic groups working within the food, agriculture, hospitality and construction industries. Most migrant workers are young and highly productive workers, meeting shortfalls in different industries and providing the labour and skills that Northern Ireland needs. For example, in the past few years immigrants from Eastern Europe have provided valuable labour within the construction industry.

Other more established **ethnic minority** groups that have been in Northern Ireland for many years have set up their own businesses, helping to generate more income and provide much needed jobs for local communities.

Finally, anyone who works in Northern Ireland has to pay taxes to fund public services and therefore contributes to the economy in this way.

Activity

4. Design a concept map to show how Northern Ireland is enriched by different ethnic minorities and influences from other countries.

Key words
ethnic minority ▪ immigrant

Conflict

As well having benefits there are also many challenges of living in a multicultural society – conflict can arise between people of different ethnic origins or religious and political beliefs.

For example, religious differences can cause a great deal of conflict as people depend on their religious views for their sense of identity and belonging. If one group considers its views to be superior to another then this can cause conflict. Some examples of where religious conflict has arisen around the world include:

■ The ongoing conflict in the Middle East between Israel (Jews) and Palestine (Muslims) over land they feel they have a religious and historical right to.

■ The conflict in India between Hindus and Muslims which led to the division of India, in 1947, into two separate countries – India and Pakistan.

Conflict in Northern Ireland

Another area of the world which has seen religious and political conflict is, of course, Northern Ireland.

The two main cultural groups in Northern Ireland (Unionist/Protestant and Nationalist/Catholic) each have their own long established and separate traditions which are based on their religious/political views.

In Northern Ireland, most Catholics consider themselves to be Irish and are nationalistic in their political view. They would like to see a united Ireland which is independent from Britain. In contrast, most Protestants in Northern Ireland consider themselves to be British; they are unionist in their political outlook and want to remain part of the United Kingdom. A lack of understanding and respect for each other's different identities and political views has led to conflict in the past.

> It is important to remember that as a result of the Belfast /Good Friday Agreement, citizens in Northern Ireland can choose to have both a British and Irish passport. This means that people can have dual nationality (British/Irish), however most prefer to maintain either a British or Irish identity.

Many aspects of cultural identity such as music, sport and flags have been used by both traditions to maintain their own identities (see pages 6–7). These signs and symbols have often served to separate the two communities and as a result reinforce people's view of themselves as belonging to one or other group.

Segregated housing and schooling where Catholics and Protestants live in separate areas and go to separate schools have helped to keep the two main communities apart. This has resulted in there being very few opportunities for the two sides to mix, which prevents them from getting to know one another, breaking down barriers and moving away from stereotypes and **prejudices** they have learned.

Sectarianism

One of the challenges which is faced by a country where there is conflict because of differences in religious beliefs is **sectarianism**. Sectarianism means having a strong and narrow-minded dislike towards another religion and rejecting those who do not share the same beliefs. This strong intolerance towards another religion can lead to prejudice, **discrimination** and even violence.

Sectarianism has been a major problem in Northern Ireland. It has led to periods of conflict between Nationalist/Catholics and Unionist/Protestants such as 'The Troubles'.

Activity

1. Using the case study on page 11 and your own knowledge, answer the following questions.

   a) Identify and explain **one** way in which sectarianism is being 'kept alive' in Northern Ireland.

   b) Identify and explain **two** ways in which Northern Ireland has become a segregated society.

   c) Identify and explain the **two** reasons given in the case study for the cause of sectarianism.

   d) Identify and explain **two** ways in which attitudes are changing in Northern Ireland.

   e) With reference to the case study and your own knowledge, evaluate the ways the government can help to end sectarianism in Northern Ireland.

The Troubles began in 1969 with widespread sectarian violence and lasted for over 30 years. It was a violent period in Northern Ireland's history, where the rule of law was not always upheld and human rights were abused.

During this period over 3500 people were killed and many more injured or left homeless.

Case study

Sectarianism and changing attitudes

Sectarianism has been part of life in Northern Ireland since the early twentieth century. It continues to be kept alive by older generations in each community who speak of past atrocities and hurts. Few, if any, parts of Northern Ireland life escape the sectarian attitudes and behaviour which exist between Protestants and Catholics.

Violence, intimidation and discrimination have created a segregated society in Northern Ireland. Latest crime figures from the PSNI show that in 2009/10 sectarian crime was up by more than 24 per cent compared with the previous year.

▲ Sectarian violence in Belfast demonstrates that deep-rooted divisions still exist in Northern Ireland. This photograph shows nationalist protesters in North Belfast in July 2010.

Some say religion is responsible for the separated and divided society, others say it is politics. Whatever the reasons, sectarianism promotes bitterness and, as we see in the history of Northern Ireland, this bitterness often leads to violence and death.

Despite these worrying figures, the majority of the population support the **peace process** and want to see an end to sectarian behaviour. This was demonstrated in the overwhelming support for the **Good Friday**/Belfast **Agreement** which was signed in 1998. The Agreement was a major political breakthrough for the peace process in Northern Ireland and as a result the Northern Ireland Assembly with devolved legislative powers was established.

The entire Agreement was posted to every household in Northern Ireland and put to a **referendum** in May 1998; a referendum was also held in the Republic of Ireland. In Northern Ireland 71 per cent of people voted 'yes' in accepting the Agreement and in the Republic of Ireland 94 per cent voted 'yes' in agreeing to change their constitution in line with the Agreement.

Attitudes in Northern Ireland are also changing. In the Northern Ireland Life and Times survey (2008) the majority of people were in support of a shared future, for example:

- 80 per cent of people, if they had a choice, would prefer to live in a mixed religion neighbourhood area.
- 92 per cent would prefer to work in a mixed religion workplace.
- 70 per cent would prefer a mixed religion school for their children.

The government of Northern Ireland is also committed to building a shared and integrated society where tolerance and equality are the main priorities. The two political traditions of unionism and nationalism have agreed to work together in government. Laws which are passed take a cross-community dimension to ensure there is equality of opportunity for all. All laws must recognise that there are two clear religious/political traditions in Northern Ireland.

Key word

discrimination ▪ Good Friday Agreement ▪ peace process ▪ prejudice ▪ referendum ▪ sectarianism

Racism

Religion is not the only cause of conflict within our society. Problems can also arise when different groups consider themselves superior to other groups because of their skin colour or ethnic origin; this is called racism. An example of racism can be seen in the Apartheid case study on page 18. In simple terms, racism is where one group of people are treated less favourably than another, usually because of their skin colour. It occurs as a result of **stereotyping** and prejudice. Discrimination on the grounds of race is illegal (See page 22, *Race Relations Order 1997*). It is also illegal to be involved in any activity which could result in racism, or encouraging others to be racist ('inciting racial hatred'). However, despite the law, racism and discrimination still exist in our society. The diagram below shows how prejudice can lead to racism and discrimination.

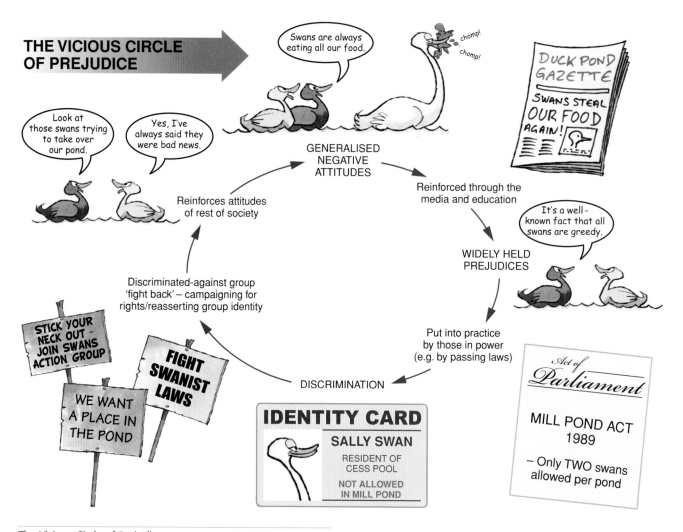

The Vicious Circle of Prejudice.

Activities

1. 'Racism is man's gravest threat to man – the maximum of hatred for the minimum of reason', Abraham J. Heschel (Jewish Theologian and Philosopher, 1907–1972). Can you explain in your own words what you think this quote means? Join with a partner and discuss your answer.

2. Look at the cartoon 'The Vicious Circle of Prejudice' on page 12. This illustrates how stereotyping, discrimination and prejudice create problems in society, which can lead to conflict between different communities. Now answer the questions below.

   a) What point is the cartoon trying to make?

   b) Working in pairs, substitute the swans for other people, and the food for jobs. Can you see any similarities between this and our society?

   c) Explain how we can end the 'The Vicious Circle of Prejudice' as:
   - **i.** an individual
   - **ii.** a society
   - **iii.** a government.

3. Look at the speech bubbles below. In small groups, discuss why you think stereotypes such as these can lead to acts of discrimination or violence. Elect a chairperson to report back to the rest of the class.

4. Identify and explain the similarities and differences between racism and sectarianism.

5. Identify and explain **one** cause of discrimination in society.

6. Identify and explain **one** equal opportunities law.

Key word
stereotyping

Immigrants come here to get benefits and don't contribute anything to the country.

Immigrants are coming over here and are taking our jobs – making us unemployed.

Blacks and Asians are responsible for most of the crime in the UK.

How serious is the problem of racism in Northern Ireland?

The two articles below from the *Belfast Telegraph* illustrate the problem of racism in Northern Ireland.

Source A

Ethnic minorities new NI victims

Wednesday 23 December 2009

Ethnic minorities have become the new victims in Northern Ireland following the end of the Troubles, the head of a migrants' group claimed. Patrick Yu said ugly scenes this year when 113 Roma Romanians were forced from their south Belfast homes were part of a growing spiral of violence against vulnerable workers and families.

There were 771 racist crimes last year, fewer than the number of sectarian incidents but on the increase. Most involved criminal damage or assaults.

More than 100 immigrants returned to Romania after the June attacks, which made headlines around the world. Vandalism left twenty terrified families staying in a church hall one night after leaving their homes.

Source B

Northern Ireland unites against racism

By David McKittrick
Thursday 18 June 2009

… Northern Ireland has made considerable efforts to combat racism. Within the past decade, funding for anti-racist initiatives has been increased, new laws have been brought in, and representatives from across the political spectrum have condemned racist attacks.

Nearly all those involved in anti-racist work agree that the attacks do not have mass support in local communities and normally involve a small number of local youths. Until the last decade, little attention was paid to the type of low-level racism endured by immigrants such as Belfast's long-established Chinese community.

Most often they involved attacks on individuals or on homes, sometimes involving the use of petrol bombs.

Those affected included blacks, Chinese, Portuguese, Filipinos, Lithuanians, Poles and Muslims and though the law, and society in general, have combined to combat racist attacks – and may well have reduced them – the bottom line is that gangs of lawless youths can still seriously harm the lives of migrant families.

Activity

7. Using Sources A and B and your own knowledge, answer the following questions.

   a) Name the nationality of the families who left their homes in Belfast in June 2009.

   b) Name **two** other ethnic minority groups who have been affected by the racism in Northern Ireland described in Source B.

   c) Identify and explain the different types of attacks on ethnic minorities described in the sources.

   d) Identify and explain **three** ways Northern Ireland has tried to deal with the problem of racism as stated in Source B.

   e) Explain the phrase 'anti-racist initiatives'.

   f) With reference to **Source B and** your own knowledge, **evaluate** the ways the government deals with issues such as racism.

Conflict resolution

As we have discovered, conflict can arise as a result of sectarian and racist behaviour. In a fair and equitable society these issues need to be resolved in a peaceful and positive way. Conflict can be resolved in different ways such as using mediation or through boycotts and sanctions.

International methods of conflict resolution

Peacekeeping

One organisation that is well known for peacekeeping and resolving conflict is the United Nations (the UN). It is an international organisation which works in countries around the world where there is political tension or unrest.

The UN was formed in 1945 after the Second World War and in 2010 it had 192 member states. Its role is to keep peace by sending international security forces into countries where there has been conflict. It tries to solve disputes peacefully, tackle the causes of conflict and promote a more peaceful society by disarming or outlawing weapons of mass destruction.

Activity

1. **a)** Using the Internet to help you, research one of the operations that the UN is currently involved in and outline how it is building peace or resolving conflict in that country. You can find out where the UN currently has peacekeeping missions at www.un.org/en/peacekeeping.

   b) Compare your research with one other person and list the similarities and differences between the two campaigns.

Although the UN does not enforce laws it does have a General Assembly which is like a parliament for all the member states. Its central aim is to preserve world peace and improve people's lives. Its work covers many different areas of life such as:

■ peace and security

■ human rights

■ humanitarian affairs

■ international law

■ economic and social development.

▲ This photograph shows UN peacekeepers handing out schoolbags to local children to mark the International Children's Day in Bukavu in the east of the Democratic Republic of Congo (DRC) in June 2009.

The UN has sent peacekeeping forces to many countries around the world including Africa, Asia and Europe to try to resolve conflict through peaceful means.

In solving a conflict or disagreement in a particular country, the use of peacekeeping forces is not always the best solution and other methods of conflict resolution such as mediation, international law, sanctions and boycotts are used.

Mediation

This is an informal negotiation with an independent, neutral, third party (the mediator) who helps to solve disputes or disagreements between two or more groups of people. It is important to remember that the mediator does not take sides, their job is to help the parties involved in a dispute come together to negotiate until they reach agreement.

In mediation, each person or group is given the opportunity to explain their views and how they relate to the conflict; both sides listen to each other's points of view.

The ultimate goal is for each side or group to understand or empathise with the other person's point of view. This helps to build trust and is an essential part of the mediation process. The UN also has full-time mediators who work in areas where there is conflict to try to prevent further disagreements and to ease tension where there is political unrest.

In 2010, the US and UN were involved in re-establishing direct talks between the Israelis and the Palestinians. Another example where mediation has been successful is the Peace Process in Northern Ireland.

International Human Rights Instruments

In democratic countries human rights are protected by governments to ensure that everyone is treated fairly and given equal opportunities in life. These governments sign International Human Rights Instruments to protect their citizens and to make sure that their own laws do not contradict international laws.

International Human Rights Instruments are laws that governments must keep. They are made up of various international human rights documents such as the **United Nations Convention on the Rights of the Child (UNCRC)** and the **Universal Declaration of Human Rights (UDHR)**. Governments that sign these declarations have made a commitment to make sure that their own laws agree with these international laws. They protect people's human rights and also shape the law in the countries that have signed them. In a country where there is war or conflict, people can sometimes have their rights abused. International Human Rights Instruments are there to protect everyone's rights and to make sure that the government is doing all it can to abide by these international laws.

However, not everyone has their human rights protected. In countries which are run by dictators, such as North Korea, there are many examples of human rights abuses. These governments are known as 'dictatorships'.

South Africa experienced conflict during **Apartheid** where people were not treated equally (see page 18). The government did not follow international human rights law and so failed to protect its citizens' human rights.

The judicial system

Conflict can arise in society between groups or individuals and the judicial system or law is there to help resolve conflicts which arise and protect people's rights.

The 'courts' are often considered the third branch of government, and the judicial power they have is a crucial part of political stability in society. The courts provide a channel through which disputes among citizens, or disputes between the state and its citizens, can be settled in a peaceful and constructive manner.

Northern Ireland has its own **judicial system** which is there to protect individuals and to promote equality and fairness within society. The law brings order to a society with rules and regulations which are there for our safety; it also protects us from harm and promotes orderly living for everyone.

The Human Rights Act 1998 meant that the European Convention on Human Rights was built into UK law for the first time. All laws which are passed in the UK and in the Northern Ireland Assembly must abide by the Human Rights Act 1998 and the European Convention on Human Rights.

The Human Rights Act includes rights such as:

- right to a fair trial
- freedom of thought
- respect for family life
- freedom of expression.

The law helps to resolve conflict peacefully and is also there to protect people's rights. For example, if a person feels that they have been treated unfairly at work they can take their employer to court or if someone has committed a crime against another person they can use the law to resolve the conflict and report the incident to the police.

Sanctions and boycotts

Sanctions and boycotts are most often used by governments that are trying to change the behaviour of another government without using violence. They are a peaceful way of trying to change the behaviour of an offending party, by punishing them economically, socially or politically. Two examples of the use of sanctions can be found in the case study on page 18.

Sanctions and boycotts are either imposed by individual governments or by governments acting together through the UN. For example, if a country is considered guilty of committing human rights abuses, the governments of other countries might:

- ban exports from that country, which means they will refuse to buy any products or goods from that country (boycott)
- withhold aid or loans (sanctions).

This is intended to put pressure on the offending country to change.

Key words

Apartheid ▪ judicial system ▪ United Nations Convention on the Rights of the Child (UNCRC) ▪ Universal Declaration of Human Rights (UDHR)

Case study

The use of sanctions in South Africa and Iraq

South Africa

An example where sanctions and boycotts were used successfully is in the case of South Africa. From 1948 until 1994 the National Government of South Africa enforced a system of legal racial segregation known as Apartheid. This was a system of government where a minority white government were in power over a majority non-white population.

Rights of the non-white majority were limited and there was widespread discrimination and inequality. For example, whites and non-whites were not allowed to travel in the same railway carriages or sit in the same seats on buses. It was also illegal for whites and non-whites to marry. Other examples of government-enforced segregation could be seen in education, medical care and public service, with blacks and non-whites receiving services inferior to those of white people.

Apartheid was internationally recognised as racist and unjust by the international community and in the 1980s boycotts and economic sanctions were introduced by different governments to put pressure on the South African government to end Apartheid. For example, banks refused to continue lending money to South Africa and sanctions were introduced.

Sports teams boycotted South Africa, with football, rugby, cricket and other teams refusing to play in the country. South Africa was banned from taking part in international competitions such as the football World Cup, until they ended Apartheid.

Sanctions did not bring a sudden end to Apartheid as they did not cover everything and South Africa had plenty of raw materials and continued to export products such as coal, iron and gold that other countries needed. However, international action did help in pressurising the South African government into talking to the African National Congress (ANC), a political group fighting for equal rights for blacks and whites in South Africa, and in securing the release from prison of a leader of the ANC, Nelson Mandela.

Apartheid finally came to an end in 1994 when the multi-racial elections took place and were won by the ANC, making Nelson Mandela President of South Africa.

▲ Even the beaches were racially segregated; non-whites were not permitted to swim or sunbathe in the same areas as the white community.

Iraq

The use of sanctions and boycotts can sometimes have a damaging effect on the citizens of a country and are not always successful in resolving conflict. Sanctions were used to prevent Iraq from developing or maintaining weapons of mass destruction after the first Iraq war (1991). Sanctions imposed by the United Nations Security Council resulted in a limited supply of food and medical supplies for the population, which caused serious hardship for ordinary Iraqi citizens, especially children.

According to **UNICEF** there was an increase in the number of child deaths during the period that sanctions were introduced, with estimates of a 500,000 increase in child deaths. Other estimates suggest that there were up to 1.7 million child casualties in total, as a result of sanctions and war.

One of the reasons for this was a lack of clean water. Chlorine manufacture was banned and imports were restricted as it was considered to be a chemical which could be used to make weapons. This led to disease and, with a shortage of medical supplies, many Iraqi people suffered during this period.

Although it is widely accepted that sanctions had a devastating effect across the whole country, the number of deaths and illnesses related to the sanctions were much lower in the north where the UN was in charge of the relief programme compared with the south where Saddam Hussein was in charge.

Economic sanctions were not successful in removing the Iraqi dictator from power and in fact probably helped to strengthen his position as many of the Iraqi people blamed the UN for their situation and looked to their dictator Saddam Hussein for help.

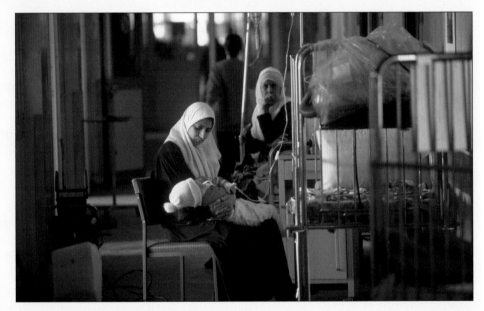

▲ Sanctions led to a shortage of milk and medical supplies during the Iraq war and many children died as a result of this.

Activities

Using the information in the case study, answer the following questions.

2. How successful were sanctions and boycotts in helping to bring an end to Apartheid in South Africa?

3. Identify and explain **two** reasons why sanctions were not successful in Iraq.

4. In groups, discuss how sanctions and boycotts could be used in a more successful way to put pressure on governments who are not treating their citizens fairly.

5. In groups, discuss the differences between the two examples where sanctions were used – South Africa and Iraq – and list **two** similarities and **two** differences.

Key words

UNICEF

Local methods of conflict resolution

As well as the international methods outlined on pages 15–17 there are many other ways communities and groups try to resolve conflict.

Conflict resolution in Belfast

Northern Ireland is a community in transition; a country emerging from over 30 years of conflict and unrest which have had a negative impact on society. Communities have been pulled apart and completely segregated with many still divided in terms of housing and schools.

For many people in Northern Ireland, differences in identity or background have been seen as a threat, rather than something to be celebrated or valued. Even today, despite the peace process, many young people continue to experience the reality of sectarianism and racism.

During the Troubles one of the worst affected areas was Belfast, which still experiences difficulties today in terms of rioting in 'interface' areas. Organisations such as the Belfast Conflict Resolution Consortium (BCRC) are involved in dealing with conflict resolution in the city and trying to promote inclusion and peace.

As part of their work, the BCRC focuses on **interface areas** in an attempt to ease tension and resolve conflict between the two main communities. Their aim is to try to understand why the barriers still exist which prevent different communities from coming together.

One of the strategies they use in promoting peace and resolving conflict is to provide opportunities for the two main traditions to come together, build positive relationships and work together in the interests of both communities. Their aim is that both communities will resolve their difficulties and collaborate on issues which affect them such as health, the economy and the environment.

The BCRC and other community groups play a valuable part in helping Northern Ireland to move from conflict and the legacy of a violent past to a future of peace and prosperity.

Non-Governmental Organisations (NGOs)

Northern Ireland has a wide range of **NGOs** that work with different groups in the community. Some of these groups focus on resolving difficulties which have arisen between different groups.

The Community Relations Council (CRC)

One of the most important NGOs, in terms of resolving conflict in Northern Ireland, is the Community Relations Council which was set up to promote good relations between the two main communities in Northern Ireland as well as promoting inclusion for ethnic minorities. Its main aim is to promote peace, reconciliation and mutual trust by:

Activity

6. Evaluate the role of the Community Relations Council in resolving conflict in Northern Ireland.

- providing support (financial, training, advice) for local groups and community organisations
- providing opportunities for cross-community projects to build trust and understanding in the community.

It also works with other organisations to help them develop good community relations and encourage greater acceptance of and respect for cultural diversity. Many of the groups that they support work within local communities trying to find peaceful ways of resolving disputes and conflict.

Northern Ireland Council for Ethnic Minorities (NICEM)

NICEM supports people from ethnic minorities in Northern Ireland by raising awareness of problems that affect them such as bullying or harassment. It tries to ensure that the law does not exclude them or have a negative effect on their needs.

It provides an important interpreting service for people who do not speak English and enables ethnic minorities to settle disputes and disagreements peacefully.

You will not be examined on the work of NICEM but an awareness of what the organisation does is helpful for your understanding of this topic.

Individuals and conflict resolution

What can individuals do to resolve conflict peacefully?

To build a better future together we need to build positive relationships with one another. This is achieved through having respect for one another and recognising and celebrating our differences. It is also important that as individuals we are aware of our own prejudices and stereotypes and that we are prepared to challenge behaviour which is inappropriate – for example, if someone is racist or sectarian.

We can also take part in community projects, lobby our local councillors/ **Members of the Legistlative Assembly (MLAs)** and even volunteer to work with NGOs that work within different communities to resolve disputes and disagreements.

Activities

9. In groups of four, think of all the strategies you have looked at for dealing with conflict in society and discuss which methods you think would be the most successful.

10. Can you think of any other ways of dealing with conflict in society?

Activities

7. Explain **two** ways minority groups could experience conflict in Northern Ireland.

8. Identify and explain **two** ways NICEM could help minority groups to resolve these conflicts.

Key words

interface areas ■ NGOs (Non-Government Organisations) ■ MLAs

Promoting inclusion

In a multicultural society, it is important that everyone is included and that differences between culture are respected. This is necessary in order to build a cohesive society, that is, one where there is harmony, mutual understanding and equality for all.

How can we promote an **inclusive** society where no one is left out and everyone is treated equally? What can we do to stop racism and sectarianism and put an end to the vicious circle of prejudice? One of the most effective and successful ways of making sure that everyone is included and that everyone receives their basic human rights is to pass laws to make discrimination on the grounds of colour, ethnic origin or religion illegal.

The law

Promoting a fair and inclusive society means having laws in place which are just and which can promote equality and help to end discrimination.

One of the most important laws in Northern Ireland is the *Race Relations Order 1997* which was passed in order to protect people from being discriminated against on the grounds of race. This law is important because it also made it illegal to encourage others to become racist or act in a racist way ('inciting racial hatred').

After the Good Friday/Belfast Agreement was signed in 1998 the government made a promise to its citizens that it would be committed to promoting equality of opportunity for all its citizens. As a result, Section 75 of the *Northern Ireland Act (1998)* was passed. This law means that it is compulsory for government authorities such as the Department of Education, Department of Health, Social Services and Public Safety, the Housing Executive, the Police Service of Northern Ireland (PSNI) and other public bodies to *actively promote equality*.

Section 75 states that government and public bodies must promote equality between people of different:

- religious groups
- ages
- racial groups
- marital status
- sexual orientation
- gender
- political opinion

▲ Parliament Buildings in Stormont, Belfast, where our politicians meet to discuss the important issues which affect us all. This is also where they introduce new laws.

and between persons:

■ with or without a disability
■ with or without dependents (children or older people they look after).

Public bodies must also promote good relations between people of different racial groups, religion or political opinion.

Giving people their rights helps to ensure that they have protection from discrimination. Ensuring that policies and practice actively promote equality provides citizens with a sense of security and a guarantee that their rights will be protected.

Another way that the government tries to promote inclusion is by providing funding for projects which bring the two main communities together through cross-community projects.

Inclusion

As well as having laws to protect people from inequality it is also important to promote inclusion in society. This can be done through schools, in the community and in the workplace.

Promoting inclusion in schools

In schools there are lots of different pupils with different needs and backgrounds. Some have specific learning difficulties, physical disabilities, some speak English as an additional language, and some have different religious and cultural backgrounds. It is important that all pupils feel included in school life and are respected.

Schools provide excellent opportunities for pupils to learn the importance of accepting others who are different. Pupils can be encouraged to respect the differences in others and to promote the importance of human rights. Schools have inclusion policies and bullying policies in place to try to avoid pupils feeling excluded and discriminated against.

In addition to the formal policies and curriculum the school has in place, there are other activities that schools can do to promote diversity and inclusion such as:

■ Hold a celebration of culture day. For example, on the European Day of Languages pupils could carry out research into the different languages which are spoken in Northern Ireland, or sample different foods from different countries.
■ Organise special assemblies focusing on cultural diversity.
■ Provide food in the canteen catering for different dietary needs.
■ Ensure that after-school clubs include pupils who have a disability.

Activities

1. What activities does your school do to promote diversity and inclusion? Research the different strategies that are already in place in your school to make sure that all pupils are treated fairly and that all pupils are included.

2. Individually or in pairs, look at the following groups of pupils who may not feel included in school life and try to think of ways that these pupils could be included fully in the life of the school:

   a) pupils with a physical disability

   b) pupils with learning difficulties

   c) pupils with English as an additional language

   d) pupils from different religions.

3. Discuss why is it so important to make sure that *all* pupils are given the same opportunities.

Key words

inclusive ■ Section 75

Activities

4. Read Source A and answer the following questions.

   a) Who is responsible for organising the Midnight Soccer Project?

   b) Identify and explain the main purpose of the Midnight Soccer Project.

   c) With reference to **Source A and** your own knowledge **evaluate** how successful projects like this can be in helping to reduce racist and sectarian behaviour in the local community.

5. Using the information in the case study opposite and your own knowledge, answer the following questions.

   a) **Who** can contact the Equality Commission for help?

   b) **What** is the main purpose of the Equality Commission?

   c) **Where** is the Equality Commission based?

   d) **Why** was the Equality Commission formed?

   e) **When** do people go to the Equality Commission for help?

Promoting inclusion within the local community

Local communities play an important role in helping to shape how society thinks. For example, if a community is welcoming to ethnic minorities, young people in that community will learn tolerance and acceptance of others who are different from themselves. Local community groups, such as the one featured in Source A, are an example of how to build good relations within the community. This particular project was aimed at challenging racism and sectarianism in the local community, and helping to build a more inclusive society.

Source A

Midnight Street Soccer helps tackle racism in Castlereagh

Approximately 60 young people in Castlereagh have been exploring the impact of racism in society during a two-week session of the popular Midnight Street Soccer league. Participants received a training session on anti-racism and sectarianism, and took part in a kick-about session with the Irish Football Association's (IFA) intercultural team World United.

Funded by the Community Safety Partnership, Midnight Street Soccer is a weekly football league for girls and boys aged thirteen to seventeen years old.

It is a community football programme which uses sport as a way to engage young people, increase participation, reduce anti-social behaviour and build positive relationships between young people in different communities.

It aims to challenge sectarian attitudes and create an understanding of cultures and identities for the young people involved.

Trainer Davey White used a mix of interactive games and personal stories to encourage the young people of Cregagh to be tolerant of others and take a stand if they see discrimination in their communities.

Following the two-week session the IFA intercultural team World United met the Midnight Soccer players for an informal chat about their background in football and cultural differences in their home country – World United boasts a wealth of talented players from Northern Ireland, Portugal, Zimbabwe, France, Ivory Coast and Poland.

The *Belfast Telegraph*

Promoting inclusion within the workplace

As we have learned, there are laws in place to protect people from discrimination and to promote inclusion. For example, the Equal Pay Act (1970) makes it illegal to discriminate on the grounds of gender regarding pay and conditions. Other laws (see the case study on page 25) make it illegal to discriminate on the grounds of religion, sexual orientation, race, age, ethnicity and against those with a disability.

Employers also have a legal responsibility to provide a safe and healthy working environment for their employees.

Case study

Equality Commission for Northern Ireland

The Equality Commission for Northern Ireland (ECNI) is an independent public body which was set up to promote equality and tackle discrimination in Northern Ireland. It gives free advice to individuals, businesses and public bodies on equality issues and, in some circumstances, has powers to investigate complaints which have been reported.

If someone feels that they have been treated unfairly, they can contact the ECNI where they will be given information about their rights under anti-discrimination law. The Commission may also be able to provide legal assistance for some complaints.

The ECNI is responsible for giving advice based on current laws such as:

- Equal Pay Act (Northern Ireland) 1970 (as amended)
- Sex Discrimination (Northern Ireland) Order 1976 (as amended)
- Disability Discrimination Act 1995 (as amended)
- Race Relations (Northern Ireland) Order 1997 (as amended)
- Fair Employment and Treatment (Northern Ireland) Order 1998 (as amended)
- Northern Ireland Act 1998

- Equality (Disability, etc.) (Northern Ireland) Order 2000
- Employment Equality (Sexual Orientation) Regulations (Northern Ireland) 2003
- Employment Equality (Age) Regulations (Northern Ireland) 2006.

Below are two examples of campaigns that the Equality Commission was recently involved in.

▲ This campaign was to inform the public about changes to the law. The Equality Act (Sexual Orientation) Regulations (Northern Ireland) 2006 came into force on 1 January 2007 and makes it unlawful to discriminate on grounds of sexual orientation in the provision of goods, facilities and services, education and public functions. Previously the law only applied to employment and vocational training.

▲ This campaign was called 'What Colours Your Judgement?' Its aim was to raise awareness that racial discrimination is unlawful and affects the chances of young people now and in the future.

Section 2 Rights and responsibilities regarding local, national and global issues

Learning outcomes

I am learning about:

* the ways I can become more aware of and active in local, national and global issues
* the importance of the Universal Declaration of Human Rights (UDHR).

In this section you will consider how to become more aware of and active in local, national and global issues; for example, through involvement in pressure groups and volunteering. You will also examine different articles from the Universal Declaration of Human Rights (UDHR) to gain a better understanding of their importance in promoting equality in our society.

What is social responsibility?

Social responsibility is when individuals and groups within society commit themselves to making a difference to the lives of others and have a genuine concern about the welfare of others. People who are socially responsible also care about the rights of others. They make a stand and speak out for those who are discriminated against or treated unfairly. When people choose to be socially responsible, they are helping to bring about justice and equality for all.

Many high-profile celebrities such as Brad Pitt, Angelina Jolie and Bono have used their fame and celebrity status to help improve the lives of other people across the world and are examples of people who are socially responsible.

FIRST THEY CAME for the Communists, and I didn't speak up because I wasn't a Communist.
THEN THEY CAME for the trade unionists, and I didn't speak up because I wasn't a trade unionist.
THEN THEY CAME for the Jews, and I didn't speak up because I wasn't a Jew.
THEN THEY CAME for the Catholics, and I didn't speak up because I wasn't a Catholic.
THEN THEY CAME for me and by that time there was no one left to speak up for me.

A famous poem attributed to Pastor Niemoller, a prominent anti-Nazi German pastor. It shows why it is important to be concerned about the welfare and rights of others, and that when we protect other people's rights we also protect our own.

Activities

1. Read the case study on page 27 about Bono's work. Choose one of the organisations that he has helped to create and research it. Find out about the work it does and how it helps people in need.

2. Read the poem opposite carefully and then explain what point you think the poem is trying to make.

Case study

Bono

'Celebrity is currency, so I wanted to use mine effectively.' Bono

Bono is most famous for being the lead singer of the Dublin-based rock band U2. He has used his position of fame and celebrity to influence governments and raise awareness of many problems around the world such as Third World debt and the Aids pandemic in Africa.

He has been nominated for the Nobel Peace prize, has been voted 'Man of the Year' by *Time* magazine and has been internationally recognised for his humanitarian work.

Bono was involved in the Band Aid and Live Aid projects and later helped organise the 2005 Live 8 project; rock concerts which were run in order to raise funds for developing countries.

He has been a leader in the fight against poverty, helping to create different organisations and campaigns to fight extreme poverty and preventable diseases, mainly in Africa. Examples of these include the ONE Campaign, which was set up to fight poverty and disease; DATA (Debt Aid Trade Africa);

and EDUN, a clothing company which is striving to encourage trade with poverty-stricken countries.

He has met presidents and other world leaders to try to change how they respond to poverty in developing countries and to influence them to work harder to help those who live in countries where there is a poor quality of life for many.

He continues to work to improve the lives of millions of people across the world through his various humanitarian campaigns.

Famous people such as Bono may find it easier to bring about change in our society because of their celebrity status. However, that is no reason to give up and say 'I am only one person, what could I do to change society?' or, 'Who would listen to me?'

Many individuals make a difference every day and we can all play our part; we may not be able to change the world, but we can change the world for at least one person. For example, individuals such as Nelson Mandela, Gandhi or Martin Luther King helped to promote equality and social justice in society, and others such as Mother Teresa made a difference to people living in poverty or disease.

Key word

social responsibility

▲ Irish singer and activist Bono receives the 2007 Liberty Medal in recognition of his humanitarian work.

How can we be socially responsible?

There are many different ways in which individuals can contribute to society. Below are some examples.

Volunteering

▲ Many people volunteer and give up their time to work with charities and voluntary organisations such as Age Concern, Oxfam and Barnardos. These organisations rely on volunteers. This photograph shows volunteers promoting the Oxjam music festival.

Donating

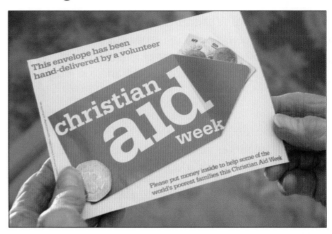

▲ Many people have changed the lives of others around the world through giving donations to charity. Charities and NGOs such as Trocaire, Christian Aid and the Red Cross rely on funding from the public to carry out their work and continue to help end suffering by bringing short- and long-term aid to developing countries.

Contacting politicians

▲ Raising issues with your local MP, councillors and MLAs is an important way of making them aware of local issues in order to support change – for example, asking them to provide better sports facilities for young people in the area, or discussing issues such as anti-social behaviour.

Signing petitions

▲ Everyone can play their part in improving the lives of others even in simple ways such as signing a petition to show their support for a particular cause. Governments risk being voted out of power if they don't listen to the voice of the people. This photo shows someone signing the 'Make Poverty History' petition. In Northern Ireland thousands of people signed a petition to prevent water rates from being introduced and they were successful in their campaign.

Joining a peaceful protest

▲ Individuals can take part in demonstrations and peaceful protests to show the government that they are not happy with decisions that are being made or laws that are being passed. **Pressure groups** hold protests to raise awareness of particular issues such as anti-war rallies or protests to end Third World debt which people can choose to take part in. This photo shows anti-war demonstrators gathering in London's Trafalgar Square in March 2008 to protest against the wars in Iraq and Afghanistan.

Joining a pressure group

Pressure groups are usually NGOs like Amnesty International, Greenpeace, Oxfam and Friends of the Earth. However, not all NGOs are pressure groups, for example, Trócaire and Christian Aid are not considered to be pressure groups. The aim of pressure groups is to try to put 'pressure' on governments to influence them or persuade them to consider the group's particular cause such as ending poverty or protecting human rights.

They use some of the following methods of indirect action:

■ lobbying governments
■ running campaigns to raise awareness of issues
■ collecting funds
■ producing materials for schools to educate pupils about issues
■ taking part in and organising demonstrations
■ publicity stunts.

Some pressure groups also use methods of direct action. Direct action can include non-violent and violent activities which target individuals, groups or property. Examples of non-violent direct action include strikes, sit-ins, sabotage, vandalism and graffiti. For example, Greenpeace often uses methods of direct action such as scaling buildings and boarding boats in order to get publicity for their campaigns.

Direct action can also involve violence against others such as using explosives to destroy a laboratory where animals are used in testing.

▲ This is part of a direct action protest against building a third runway at Heathrow.

Activities

3. Name **one** way that young people can become involved in helping to improve the leisure facilities in their local community.

4. Identify and explain **one** reason why it is important to protect the rights of others.

5. Identify and explain **two** ways that pupils could become more actively involved in their schools.

6. Explain **two** ways that NGOs/pressure groups can raise awareness of their campaigns.

7. Many people volunteer to work with NGOs and pressure groups. **Evaluate** the decision of a young person who has chosen to become involved with a local pressure group.

Key words

pressure group

The Universal Declaration of Human Rights (UDHR)

In Key Stage 3 you learned that every human is entitled to certain rights. These include basic rights such as the right to life, and the right to food and clean drinking water. Other rights include education and medical care as well as the right to practise your religion and freedom of expression.

Modern human rights were developed after the Second World War, after many people's rights had been abused. The United Nations (UN) was formed in 1945 to maintain international peace and promote co-operation in solving international problems. Currently there are 192 member states.

The UDHR was signed in 1948 by the 48 member states of the UN. It was signed to protect people's rights and is a promise or commitment made by governments around the world to safeguard people's human rights. It consists of 30 Articles (declarations or promises) describing the basic rights of every person. It is important to remember that these rights are only 'promises'; that is, they are not legally binding until they become part of the law. Only when they are made law can they be considered legal rights. Two documents that were inspired by the UDHR and are legally binding are the **European Convention on Human Rights (ECHR)** and the United Nation Convention on the Rights of the Child (UNCRC).

Activity

1. Look at the rights from the UDHR listed on the right. In groups, discuss which you think are the most important and then rank them in order of importance. (You can find the full list of rights on the UDHR website www.udhr.org.)

Some UDHR rights

Everyone:

1. Is born free and should be treated equally.
2. Has the right to a home and medical care if they need it.
3. Has the right to live in freedom and safety.
4. Should be free from slavery.
5. Should have a fair trial.
6. Has the right to rest and leisure.
7. Has the right to go to school.
8. Has the right to marry.
9. Has the right to take part in government and vote.
10. Has the right to an adequate standard of living.

The European Convention on Human Rights (ECHR)

The ECHR was a treaty signed in 1950 by the then member states of the Council of Europe. Today, adherence to the convention is a condition of membership to the European Union (EU) and EU member states have a legal obligation to make sure that their citizens enjoy the rights that are laid down in the treaty.

In 1998 the Human Rights Act brought the European Convention on Human Rights into UK law.

United Nations Convention on the Rights of the Child (UNCRC)

The UNCRC is an international human rights treaty that grants all children and young people (aged seventeen and under) a comprehensive set of rights. The UK signed the Convention in 1990 and it came into force in the UK in 1992. The UNCRC is a very important document because it is specially written for children and focuses on their rights. Some of these rights include:

- The right to play
- The right to healthcare
- The right to be with their family or those who will care for them best
- The right to free education
- The right to protection from cruelty, neglect and injustice.

You will not be examined on either the ECHR or UNCRC treaties. However, an awareness of what they are is important for your understanding of the topic of human rights.

Activities

2. Look at the photographs below and explain what human rights are being violated in each.

3. How can each of the following help to protect human rights:
   a. individuals?
   b. societies?
   c. governments?

A

B

C

D

Key words
European Convention on Human Rights (ECHR)

Articles of the UDHR

The statements or declarations in the UDHR are called 'Articles' and on pages 32–42 we explore them in depth.

Life, liberty and security of the person (Article 3)

Article 3 means that people should have the right to live in freedom and safety. That is, no one has the right to take another person's life or cause them any harm.

How can we be protected in order to live in freedom and safety?

The national and local government passes laws and the police force uphold the law in order to keep us safe and make sure that we all have the rights we are entitled to. It is our responsibility to influence our governments to guarantee these rights are enjoyed by all.

There have been a number of laws passed which support Article 3. These laws have been written not just to protect people's rights but also to give the police the necessary powers to keep peace and order in society.

- Northern Ireland Act 1998 (Section 75): aims to protect minority groups from hate crime.
- Crime and Security Act (2010): aims to protect our communities by making our streets safer and giving more help to victims of crime.
- Policing and Crime Act (2009): aims to increase the effectiveness of local police forces and make them more accountable to their communities.
- Health and Safety Act (2008): aims to penalise breaches of health and safety legislation more severely.
- Criminal Justice Act (2003): provides a general framework for sentence decision-making.

The law is also there to protect us and make sure that we all have the rights we are entitled to. For example, we need to be safe on our roads or walking home at night. Laws are passed for our personal safety on the roads and the police force carry out patrols to make sure we are safe at night.

International treaties

Local and national governments also work closely with other governments across the world to ensure that everyone enjoys their right to safety and security. For example, they sign international agreements or treaties where they promise to give their citizens the protection that they are entitled to. In 1997, 133 governments signed the Ottawa Treaty which is a treaty or agreement to ban the use of landmines.

Activity

1. In small groups, discuss the ways in which Article 3 is violated in our society (for example, when someone commits a crime that affects someone else's safety and freedom). Feed back your results to the rest of the class.

Case study

Landmines

▲ Landmines continue to kill and seriously injure thousands of people around the world each year.

Although Article 3 of the UDHR states that everyone should be kept safe from harm and should be protected, sadly this is not always the case. In some countries where there has been conflict many citizens do not enjoy the safety and security that they are entitled to. In some of these war zones, landmines have been used as a weapon to protect border areas and are a very dangerous and damaging tool of war. Even after wars have ended the landmines remain in the ground causing injury and death.

- Landmines kill or maim thousands of people each year. Most are civilians. Many are children.
- Long after wars in different areas of the world have ended, the use of landmines continues to deny the right to life and liberty of large numbers of civilians.

In 1991, several NGOs and individuals began to discuss the need to co-ordinate initiatives for a ban on landmines. Governments around the world responded to the campaign by negotiating the 1997 Convention on the Prohibition of the Use, Stockpiling, Production and Transfer of Anti-Personnel Mines and on their Destruction.

The Mine Ban Treaty prohibits, in all circumstances, any use of anti-personnel landmines.

It also requires that stockpiles be destroyed within four years of the treaty's enforcement, and that mines already in the ground be destroyed within ten years. The treaty entered into force on 1 March 1999. As of April 2010, 156 countries had signed the treaty; in contrast, the United States, Russia and China are among 50 countries that so far have refused to sign the treaty. The US is believed to have a stockpile of 11.2 million landmines.

Activities

2. Explain why landmines prevent some people from living in freedom and safety.

3. Using the information in the case study, explain how successful NGOs have been in preventing landmines being used.

4. Explain why you think some countries have not signed the treaty.

Activities

5. Below are three issues where the right to privacy conflicts with another right. Work in pairs to identify the arguments in favour of each right. Then join up with another pair and prepare a class debate on one of the issues.

6. Should it be compulsory for everyone to carry identity cards?

7. Is the increased use of CCTV for our protection or an invasion of our privacy?

8. Should the media be allowed to print whatever they want – is this really freedom of expression, or does it conflict with a person's right to privacy?

▲ CCTV cameras are frequently used to monitor and record people's movements, especially in towns and cities.

Interference with privacy, family, home or correspondence (Article 12)

Article 12 of the UDHR states that everyone has 'The right to be protected if someone tries to harm your good name, enter your house, open your letters, or bother you or your family without a good reason.' Essentially it is about people's right to privacy.

This right is often in conflict with other rights; for example, the use of CCTV surveillance to prevent crime or the reading of prisoners' letters and the censoring of what they read can conflict with the right of life, liberty and security of the person.

Another example of where this right can conflict with another is the right to privacy in relation to the media.

The media and privacy

The media (television, newspapers, etc.) has the right to freedom of expression. Sometimes this can conflict with people's right to privacy, particularly when the media publish details of a person's personal life.

If someone feels that the media is violating their right to privacy, they can:

■ ask a court for an injunction to stop the story being published
■ complain to the Press Complaints Commission who can order an apology if they think the complaint is reasonable
■ seek damages if something has already been published.

The difficulty is the balance between freedom of the press and the right to privacy of the individual. Sometimes it is up to the courts to decide which right is more important. Usually the deciding factor is whether the publication of material is 'in the public interest' or not.

Celebrities often have a battle with newspapers or magazines about the right to privacy. Sometimes the court finds in favour of a celebrity and makes the newspaper or magazine pay them damages if they have invaded a celebrity's privacy or published something which wasn't true. A successful example of this is J.K. Rowling who successfully took legal action to ban publication of photographs of her son.

The right to vote (Article 21)

Article 21 of the UDHR states that 'You have the right to take part in your country's political affairs either by belonging to the government yourself or by choosing politicians who have the same ideas as you. Governments should be voted for regularly and voting should be secret. You should get a vote and all votes should be equal.'

Having the right to vote and being able to decide who runs your country is one of our most important human rights. Having a say in who runs your country is a characteristic of all modern **democratic** countries. In the UK all men and women over the age of 21 were allowed to vote in 1928. The law changed in 1969 and now all men and women (with a few exceptions, for example: foreign nationals or those held in psychiatric hospitals) are allowed to vote once they reach eighteen.

In most democracies, people can choose whether or not to vote; however, in some countries such as Australia and Brazil people must vote – this is called compulsory voting.

Do we all have the right to vote and have a say in who runs our country?

Not all countries have free and fair elections. This means that many citizens do not enjoy the freedom to choose who they want to lead them. It is estimated that there are more than 70 countries around the world which are still ruled by dictators: leaders who exercise authority over their citizens and cannot be removed by legal means.

Dictators suppress freedoms of speech and religion and the right to a fair trial. Some countries led by dictators today include Saudi Arabia, Libya, Sudan and Zimbabwe. According to Amnesty International, there are many instances of human rights abuses in these countries.

> Voting in elections gives people a 'voice': it enables them to choose a political party which they feel represents their views, and ultimately gives them a say in how their country is run.

Voting in Northern Ireland

In Northern Ireland there is a system of voting called proportional representation. This means that political parties are given a percentage of seats based on the percentage of votes they receive. If the candidates of a party win 40 per cent of the votes then they receive 40 per cent of the seats and if another party wins 20 per cent of the vote, they get 20 per cent of the seats, and so on. For example, in an area where there are ten seats and a political party receives 40 per cent of the votes then they receive four seats.

In Northern Ireland voters choose their candidates in order of preference. This system is called the Single Transferable Vote and means that voters rank the candidates in order of preference. Candidates don't need a majority of votes to be elected, just a share of the votes determined by the size of the electorate and the number of positions to be filled. If your preferred candidate has no chance of being elected or has enough votes already, your vote is transferred to another candidate in accordance with your next choice on the ballot paper.

Activity

9. Many people choose not to vote, particularly those in the 18–25 age group. List all the reasons why you think young people don't vote. Work in pairs and compare your answers then choose someone to feed back to the rest of the class.

Key words

democracy

The right to work with equal pay for equal work (Article 23)

Article 23 of the UDHR states that people should have the right to work and to earn a salary which allows them to support their family. It also states that if a man and a woman do the same work they should get the same pay.

Gender inequality

The UK government first addressed the issue of equality in the workplace in 1970 with the Equal Pay Act (Northern Ireland) (amended 1984). This act gives women and men rights to equal pay and other benefits such as holiday and sick pay. It also states that a woman should not lose her job because of pregnancy.

The government continued to address the issue of equality with the **Sex Discrimination** Act 1975 which was introduced to protect men and women from discrimination on the grounds of sex or marriage. It relates mainly to employment, education, training and the provision of goods and is there to promote equality of opportunity between the sexes.

Despite the law there are still issues of inequality in the workplace in the UK. In 2009:

> Men still earned, on average, 20 per cent more than women doing the same job.

> Only 12 per cent of top positions were held by women in the FTSE 100 companies.

> There was still a sexual division of labour where jobs are divided into 'men's jobs' and 'women's jobs', such as secretarial and nursing for women and construction and mechanical for men.

> Mothers were still responsible for the majority of childcare with many taking breaks in their careers to look after children.

> Mothers were nine times as likely as fathers to take time off to look after their children during the summer holidays.

> An estimated 440,000 women lost out on pay or promotion as a result of pregnancy.

A further example of gender inequality can be found in local and national government. After the 2010 General Election only 21 per cent of MPs in the UK government were women. In the Northern Ireland Assembly only 18 MLAs were women out of a possible 108 in the 2003 and 2007 elections.

Source A

Men still get paid more than women

The pay gap between men and women in Northern Ireland remains relatively unchanged, a major conference has been told.

A Labour Market Report produced by the Department of Enterprise, Training and Industry, referring to the period 2006–2008, confirmed that 'gender pay differences continue to exist in NI as men still earn more than women, especially in various occupational and industry groupings. The statistics were based on weekly and annual earnings trends.

'... it is also difficult to break into non-traditional sectors. There are fewer apprenticeships due to the economic situation and it seems that girls are not being given the chance to explore careers in areas such as construction, electrics, joinery and plumbing. We need to tackle these inequalities and ensure there is equal pay and equal opportunities for women.'

The *Belfast Telegraph*

Equality Act 2010

In an attempt to simplify equality legislation and to make it easier for people to understand, the government introduced new legislation with the Equality Act 2010. The Act brought together different equality laws which have been in place for several years.

Activity

10. In groups, discuss why you think many jobs are still considered 'men's' jobs and 'women's' jobs.

Adequate health and well-being for self and family (Article 25)

Article 25 looks at issues such as unemployment, poverty and homelessness. This is known as social justice or social inclusion.

It states that everyone should have adequate health and well-being for self and family. Adequate health and well-being refers to human needs such as:

- food
- clothing
- housing
- medical care
- necessary social services
- security in the event of unemployment.

Does everyone in Northern Ireland enjoy an adequate standard of living and have these basic human needs met? To answer this we need to look at what **social inclusion** and poverty mean.

Why is social inclusion important?

Everyone deserves the same opportunities in life and the same chance to enjoy different life experiences, regardless of the group they belong to or their economic circumstances. Everyone should be included in our society and, in order to ensure this, we need to give special support to those groups who need extra help, such as the elderly, the unemployed, or those living in poverty. This is social inclusion.

What is poverty?

Poverty can be defined as absolute or **relative poverty**. **Absolute poverty** is where people do not have the basic essentials such as food and shelter which they need to survive. Relative poverty is where people do not have adequate income or resources and this prevents them from enjoying a standard of living which would be regarded as acceptable by society generally.

This understanding of poverty recognises that people have social, cultural and emotional needs, as well as physical and economic needs. Living in poverty is not just about lack of money, it can also mean feeling excluded, isolated, powerless and discriminated against.

Key words

absolute poverty ■ relative poverty
■ sex discrimination ■ social inclusion

▲ Even in developed countries, like Northern Ireland, poverty is still a serious issue and the gap between the rich and poor continues to widen.

What is the situation in Northern Ireland?

In Northern Ireland there are people in society who face poverty and social exclusion. Homeless people, the unemployed, the elderly and children can be severely affected by poverty.

Homelessness

According to the Housing Executive (NIHE) the number of homeless people in Northern Ireland is on the increase, and in 2009 there were over 18,000 homeless people.

Homelessness does not simply describe people sleeping on the streets – even if you have a roof over your head you may still be homeless. For example, if your home is unsuitable for you to live in, or you have no right to stay in it, you could be classified as homeless. Being homeless really means not owning or renting a home of your own.

What can people do if they find that they have no home and nowhere to go? There are a number of NGOs which help those who are homeless. For example:

- Shelter provides long- and short-term aid to those who are experiencing housing problems. It also campaigns to ensure that the government makes housing a priority to help solve the housing shortage; in 2010 there were 1.8 million people on council waiting lists for social housing.
- One of the largest NGOs which works with the homeless is the Simon Community. It provides shelter and accommodation for young people and adults who are homeless across the UK. In Northern Ireland in 2008 there were almost 3000 young people who approached the Simon Community looking for emergency accommodation. Over half of the Simon Community residents were aged between 16 and 25.
- Centrepoint is an organisation that focuses on homeless young people. It provides short-term and long-term accommodation for young people and helps to tackle the problems that lead to homelessness.
- Crisis is a national charity for single homeless people. It provides support through housing, education and by helping them to find and keep jobs.

Activities

11. Working in pairs discuss the reasons why you think a young person could become homeless and feed back your ideas to the rest of the class.

12. Using the Internet to help you, research the work of an NGO which helps those who are homeless. Find out:

    a) when the NGO was formed

    b) how they help to improve the lives of homeless people

    c) the age range of the homeless people that they help.

Child poverty

There is a general acceptance by the government and general public that there are far too many children living in poverty.

According to the children's charity Barnardos, in 2010 there were approximately 100,000 children living in relative poverty in Northern Ireland. Many children also go without the material things and activities that their peers take for granted.

Moreover, around 44,000 children and young people are living in absolute poverty. This means they are missing out on everyday provisions that the rest of the community see as essential such as regular food and adequate housing. This inevitably leads to poor diet and poor health.

Many one-parent families also experience poverty in Northern Ireland. On the right are two examples which demonstrate some of the problems that lone parents face.

Child poverty is not just a problem in Northern Ireland and the UK but is a huge global problem. Many children living in poverty in developing countries don't have access to education, basic healthcare and essentials like food, clothing and water. The effects of this include hunger, disease and a lack of opportunities given by education. Worldwide:

- Over 25,000 children die each day from poverty and easily preventable diseases.
- 1.4 million children die each year from lack of access to safe drinking water and basic sanitation.
- There are 121 million children out of education.

My children have never been swimming; I can't afford to take them.
I want my children to be happy, well educated and to have goals. I don't want them to think or feel that they're not good enough.

Activities

13. Explain what it means to have 'access to basic sanitation'.

14. Identify and explain **two** problems that can arise from a lack of clean water.

15. Identify and explain **one** way in which NGOs/pressure groups can help those children affected by poverty.

16. Explain what we can do as individuals to help those in developing countries who do not have access to a clean water supply.

17. In groups, discuss how governments can help other countries who are suffering because their populations do not have access to clean water and proper sanitation. For example, through international aid, or by raising awareness of the problem, or by advising and sharing expertise.

I am a lone parent and have four girls aged between two and seven. I survive on £240 a week. I find it hard to cover the costs of heating, clothes and food and usually have to borrow money at the end of the week.

Unemployment

At the end of 2009 there were 54,500 people officially seeking work in Northern Ireland. Unemployment can lead to poverty, stress, divorce and homelessness for the individual which has an impact on society as a whole.

Article 25 of the UDHR states that it is a basic human right to be helped if you find yourself out of work or unable to find a job. Many governments offer support and help to those who find themselves out of work. In the UK the government has various schemes and programmes which help people back into work and also support them through benefits and training programmes such as:

- **New Deal** – a programme to help the unemployed, particularly the long-term unemployed, back to work. It provides opportunities for people to learn new skills, receive training and gain work experience.
- **Steps to Work** – provides personalised advice and guidance to help people back to work. People can retrain while still receiving benefits and a weekly training bonus. People are given opportunities to learn essential skills in Maths, English and IT.
- **Bridge to Employment** – this is a pre-employment training programme that provides skills and training to help the unemployed compete in the workplace; people are given opportunities to work in companies and gain valuable work experience.
- **Jobseeker's Allowance** – the type and amount of benefit depends on a person's circumstances and is payable to those who are actively seeking work.
- **Income Support** – for those who are on a low income or who work less than sixteen hours a week. It is also there for those who do not receive a Jobseeker's Allowance.

The government also offers other benefits to support the unemployed such as council tax benefit, housing benefit and disability allowance. Information on the various benefits and training programmes available can be found at www.direct.gov.uk and www.nidirect.gov.uk.

Activity

18. Why do you think that it is important to help those who are unemployed get back to work?

The elderly

▲ Many old people find it difficult to live on the state pension and are faced with hardship – especially during the winter months.

Another group in our society who are affected by poverty is the elderly. According to AgeUK there were at least 2.3 million pensioners living in poverty in the UK in 2009. This means that they are so poor they find it hard to heat their houses, eat nutritious food or replace household equipment. The two main causes of poverty in the elderly are: an inadequate pension which is not enough to cover basic expenses; and the fact that many older people do not claim, or are not aware of, the benefits that they are entitled to.

The problem of poverty and the elderly needs to be addressed as the aging population is steadily increasing as these estimates and projections from the Office for National Statistics, 2009, show:

Current estimates:

- There are more people over the age of 60 than under the age of eighteen.
- There are currently 12 million people of pensionable age (60 for women and 65 for men), almost one in five of the UK's total population.
- Almost 20 per cent of the population are over the age of retirement.
- There are more pensioners than there are children under the age of sixteen.

Projections:

- The number of people in the UK over 60 is expected to rise by more than 50 per cent in the next 25 years.
- The number of people over the age of 85 in the UK is predicted to double in the next twenty years and nearly treble in the next 30 years.

Having a population with such a high percentage of people over 65 brings challenges and opportunities. In a society which promotes social inclusion and 'Adequate health and well-being for all' (Article 25) we need to consider how we can care for our growing aged population. People have different opinions on how best to care for the elderly, some of these are listed below:

a. The government should raise the amount of money that pensioners are given each week.

b. The elderly should be given more help from the government in claiming the benefits they are entitled to.

c. People should save more money for their retirement and not rely heavily on the government to support them.

d. People in the community should look after the elderly more than they do; too many old people are vulnerable and left on their own.

e. Charities and NGOs could do more to help the elderly in the community.

f. People pay tax all their lives and, therefore, they should be looked after in their old age.

g. The elderly need so much care and medical attention in their old age. We need to find a system where everyone is looked after fairly.

Activities

19. Read the different opinions in the speech bubbles above and then in groups discuss whether you agree or disagree with the opinions.

20. What do you think is the best way forward in dealing with our aging population to ensure that they have adequate care provision?

Free education, at least elementary/ fundamental stages (Article 26)

Article 26 is about every child's right to go to school and the idea that primary education should be free.

It is compulsory for everyone in Northern Ireland to attend school from age five to age sixteen (unless they are being home-schooled) and local education authorities have a legal duty to ensure that free education is available to every child of compulsory school age. The education should be appropriate to the child's age, abilities, aptitudes and any special educational needs they may have.

This applies to every child who lives in the local education authority's area, whether permanently or temporarily, and therefore applies to traveller children. Education is free until the age of eighteen although it is only compulsory to stay at school until sixteen in Northern Ireland.

However, not everyone enjoys this right to free education – particularly in developing countries (see Source B).

▲ 'All children should have the opportunity to go to school and have an education.'

Source B   Education for all?

According to UNICEF, there were over 93 million children who were not in school in 2008, and more than half of these were girls. For many children, the basic human right to quality education is just a dream, an idea that has not become a reality. Although more and more children are gaining access to education and the number of out-of-school children is falling, there is still much work to be done. Children receive so many benefits from education, including acquiring skills that translate into employment and empowerment.

Education provides the knowledge, values and skills that are essential for lifelong learning and success in both life and work. Quality education is child-centred, gender-sensitive and tailored to meet the needs of different age groups. It is based on a curriculum that is relevant to the needs of all learners.

Activity

21. Read Source B and then answer the following questions.

   a. How many children around the world still do not receive a basic education?

   b. What do you think is meant by the phrase 'employment and empowerment'?

   c. According to Source B what is 'quality education'?

   d. Why do you think we do not have gender equality in education around the world?

Rights and responsibilities

As you have discovered, rights by definition are things everyone should be entitled to. We also have a responsibility to protect each other's human rights. For example:

■ You have the right to drive your car at the age of seventeen; however, you also have the responsibility to drive safely and to obey the Highway Code.

■ All children have a right to be taught and receive an education. They also have a responsibility to make sure that they attend school and that they do not prevent others from learning.

Here are some more examples of how rights carry responsibilities.

Human right	Key responsibility
We have the right to be treated in the same way and laws should apply equally to everyone (Article 7).	We should treat everyone equally. It does not matter about a person's age, gender, race, religion or sexual orientation.
Everyone is entitled to live in freedom and safety (Article 3).	We should treat everyone with respect and not do anything which would harm another individual.
Everyone is innocent until it can be proven that they are guilty. Everyone has the right to defend themselves at a public trial (Article 11).	We must listen to both sides of an argument and not jump to conclusions.

Activities

22. Which of the rights you have studied from the UDHR do you think are the most important? In groups, rank the articles in order of importance and feed back to the rest of the class. Did everyone agree on which rights were the most important?

23. Copy and complete the table below, filling in the rights with the corresponding responsibilities.

Human right	Key responsibility
Right to privacy	
Right to adequate health and well-being	
Right to vote	
Right to work and equal pay	
Right to free education	

24. Design a concept map which includes all the human rights you have looked at. A concept map is a really useful tool to use for revision and to bring together all the information on a particular topic.

Section 3 The role of society and government in safeguarding human rights

Learning outcomes

I am learning about laws relating to:

* equal opportunities

* discrimination (Section 75)

* responsibilities of the First and Deputy First Ministers of the Northern Ireland devolved government.

In this section we are going to consider what is meant by equality, how society and the government can promote equality and fairness, and how the law protects the more vulnerable groups in our society.

We will also be looking at discrimination laws and in particular Section 75 of the Northern Ireland Act (1998).

Activity

1. In groups, define 'equality'. Share your definition with the rest of the class.

Equality means that everyone should have the same opportunities in life, including access to education, leisure facilities, housing and work; no one should be excluded from any aspect of social life.

The governments of most countries in the world have signed the UDHR, showing they are committed to protecting the human rights of all their citizens, including the right to be treated equally:

'All human beings are born free and equal in dignity and rights.' (Article 1 of the UDHR)

Activities

2. Match the type of discrimination with the correct definition in the table below.

Type of discrimination	Definition
1. Homophobia	**a.** Treating an individual or group unfairly because of the colour of their skin, their race, nationality or ethnic origin.
2. Sexism	**b.** Unfair treatment because of a person's sexual orientation (gay, lesbian and transgender).
3. Racism	**c.** Discriminating against someone because of their age.
4. Ageism	**d.** Treating an individual unfairly because they have a disability.
5. Disability discrimination	**e.** Discrimination on the grounds of gender (male/female).

3. Using the table above, write down an example for each of the different types of discrimination. For example, 'Ian and Robert were turned away from staying at the B&B because they were gay.'

4. Equality is more than just treating everyone the same. In groups, discuss the question 'Is treating someone fairly the same as treating someone equally?'

Even though equality is a human right, there are still people today who are not treated equally. Inequalities can arise as a result of differences in gender, sexuality, race or disability and, as we learned earlier (see page 12), if people allow their prejudices to influence how they treat others, they are preventing them from having the same chances as everyone else. This is what is meant by discrimination and it is against the law.

In Activity 4 you may have come to the conclusion that in order to treat everyone fairly, everyone should not be treated equally. For example, there are certain groups in our society who may need extra help and support because of their material circumstances; for example, people living in poverty may need financial support with housing. Similarly, those with a disability may need more rights than those without a disability; for example, car parking rights near shops and public buildings. This ensures that no one is excluded from society and that everyone can enjoy the same opportunities as everyone else.

The law

The law is there to protect people's rights and to try to prevent discrimination. As you have already learned (page 22), one of the most important equality laws in Northern Ireland is Section 75 of the Northern Ireland Act (1998). This means that all public institutions, schools and other government organisations must make sure that certain groups in our society have access to the same opportunities as everyone else. The government has also made a commitment to actively promote equality for all minority groups in Northern Ireland.

In addition, The Equality Commission for Northern Ireland (ECNI) supports groups or individuals who feel they have not been treated equally (see page 25). The ECNI also provides advice for businesses to ensure that they are working within the law.

Key word
The Office of the First and Deputy First Ministers (OFMDFM)

The Office of the First and Deputy First Ministers (OFMDFM)

The **OFMDFM** is governed by the First and Deputy First Ministers. The First Minister is usually a member of the largest political party in the Northern Ireland Assembly and the Deputy First Minister is usually a member of the second largest party. One is usually from a Unionist party and the other is usually from a Nationalist party. The OFMDFM's range of duties include:

- overseeing the work of the other ten departments within the Assembly, and ensuring that they are carrying out their duties with the best interests of the public in mind
- overseeing all laws which are passed
- building good community relations
- building a government which makes good decisions and improves public services
- promoting equality of opportunity for all, tackling social disadvantage and meeting the needs of survivors and victims
- creating a more equal and inclusive society
- promoting and protecting the rights of everyone within Northern Ireland
- promoting investment in Northern Ireland.

Its aim is to promote a fairer and more inclusive society in Northern Ireland through supporting and liaising with the departments within the Executive.

The OFMDFM sets itself targets and plans to ensure that it delivers on the promises it makes. It has identified equality and inclusion for minority groups as one of its key priorities. These minority groups include:

- those with a different sexual orientation
- those with a disability
- racial minorities
- those living in poverty.

They have also highlighted gender equality as an area which they would like to improve in Northern Ireland.

Activity

5. Who are the current First Minister and Deputy First Minister, and what political parties do they belong to?

Section 4 Non-Governmental Organisations (NGOs)

Learning outcomes

I am learning about the role and contribution of the following NGOs:

* The Northern Ireland Council for Voluntary Action (NICVA)
* Friends of the Earth
* Oxfam
* Save the Children
* War on Want.

In this section we consider the work of several NGOs that promote equality and social justice in Northern Ireland and across the world. We examine their history, how they address different issues, such as world poverty and protecting the environment, and the aims and effectiveness of some of their campaigns.

The Northern Ireland Council for Voluntary Action (NICVA)

NICVA began in 1938 as the Northern Ireland Council for Social Services in response to high levels of unemployment in Northern Ireland. It changed its name to the Northern Ireland Council for Voluntary Action in 1986 and now represents the entire voluntary and community sector within Northern Ireland, providing organisations with support and advice on how to run successfully.

There are over 5000 **voluntary**/community **groups** in Northern Ireland, examples include: Northern Ireland Hospice Care, Advice NI, YouthNet, Gingerbread, NI Women into Politics, and Council for the Homeless NI. Voluntary and community groups played an invaluable role during the Troubles in Northern Ireland, bringing communities together and promoting peace and reconciliation. They still make a positive contribution today with many groups working in communities where there is sectarian tension and social exclusion. NICVA

protects and supports these voluntary and community groups by providing a range of other services including:

* specialist training programmes for individual organisations
* specialist advice on fundraising, training and management

Voluntary/Community

NICVA is an umbrella organisation which protects and supports voluntary and community groups.

- advice on how to select and recruit staff
- providing its members with a magazine and bulletin
- giving advice and training on charity law.

NICVA's main aim is to build a fair and equal society by supporting existing voluntary and community groups, and by helping new groups to establish themselves within the sector. In addition to the services listed above, voluntary and community groups have benefited from NICVA's guidance and support on a range of issues such as lobbying, campaigning and how to use the media effectively in raising awareness of their work.

Activity

1. Identify and explain how NICVA supports voluntary and community groups in Northern Ireland.

Friends of the Earth

Friends of the Earth was founded in 1969 in the USA and in 1971 it became an international organisation. It campaigns on urgent environmental and social issues and works towards creating a healthier environment for all. Friends of the Earth works with communities to make life better for people by inspiring solutions to environmental problems. It influences government to change policies in favour of people and the planet.

Some successes include persuading governments to:

- stop over 150 harmful dam and water projects
- ban international whaling
- consider the best legislation possible on global warming
- reform the World Bank to address environmental and human rights issues.

Key word

voluntary groups

▲ This photograph shows the Friends of the Earth's campaign for the need for clean water in Africa.

Deforestation

One of Friends of the Earth's current campaigns is to reduce deforestation which is happening on a global scale. Forests are essential to maintain a healthy planet and are a critical part of our life support system. They:

- absorb huge amounts of carbon dioxide – a climate changing gas
- keep millions of important species alive
- help prevent soil erosion
- help to provide a livelihood and food for indigenous peoples.

However, forests are disappearing at an alarming rate. Friends of the Earth estimates that we are losing an area the size of 36 football pitches per minute and, if this continues, forests could disappear completely in Indonesia by 2020. There are several reasons for this deforestation:

- **Demand for new farmland**
  Forests are cut down to grow crops like palm oil and soy. For example, the growth of oil palm plantations is driving the clearing of forests in Indonesia. Palm oil is found in many everyday goods – from muesli to toothpaste. Increasingly, it is being used as a biofuel (an alternative fuel for cars). Some governments have set targets for the use of biofuels as a way of cutting carbon dioxide emissions. However, growing crops for fuel means more land is needed and more forests are cut down. In some cases, any carbon dioxide savings made from using biofuels are wiped out when large areas of forests are destroyed.

- **Climate change**
  Rising temperatures can lead to forests dying.

▲ Deforestation is clearing a large number of trees from an area, as is shown in this photograph. It has now become a global problem.

- **Unfair trade rules**
  Big business gets easy access to timber in the developing world – and local people's rights are ignored.

Rainforest success

Friends of the Earth has been working with forest people to help them protect their rights. In Indonesia it has helped prevent 50,000 hectares of forest from being destroyed. It has also been successful in raising awareness of the problems of deforestation and now governments around the world are reconsidering their policies on the use of biofuels. It has used the media to highlight the problems of deforestation and lobbied governments to take action to prevent further destruction of the world's forests. Friends of the Earth currently has a campaign to revolutionise the food chain as much deforestation is carried out in order to grow soy, a cheap animal feed.

Activity

2. Identify and explain the different strategies that Friends of the Earth used in their campaign to protect the world's rainforests. You can research this further at www.foe.co.uk.

Oxfam

Oxfam was originally founded in 1942 as the **Ox**ford Committee for **Fam**ine relief. Today it is a worldwide charity and development agency with partners in over 100 countries. As an NGO and a pressure group, Oxfam believe there are three key ways to provide help for countries who are experiencing difficulties:

1. Emergency relief (short-term aid)

In countries where there has been war or a natural disaster such as famine or floods, Oxfam provide immediate short-term aid. They help by doing the following:

- providing clean water and sanitation in temporary camps and shelters
- providing essential items such as hygiene kits (soap, cloths and other essential items)
- sending experienced staff to help in communities where there are shortages of food.

In August 2010, Oxfam provided emergency relief for the people of Northern Pakistan when it was hit by severe floods which caused widespread devastation and left over a million people homeless. Oxfam built temporary shelters and provided essential access to clean water and sanitation facilities.

▲ In September 2009, thousands of climate change activists gathered in New York's Central Park for an event organised by Oxfam to support the 'TckTckTck' climate change campaign.

2. Development work (long-term aid)

Oxfam have a large number of development programmes in over 100 countries in the world. Their aim is to improve the lives of people by helping them to become self-supporting. They work directly with local communities on longer term projects, providing the training needed in order for these countries to manage their own development.

One of Oxfam's development programmes has been in Brazil where they have been working with local communities in North Eastern Brazil to improve access to clean water supplies. Many communities had previously only had access to clean water during the rainy season. Oxfam has helped these communities to build large concrete towers to collect the rainfall during the rainy season. This means that the people in the villages have access to water all year round and no longer have to walk several miles to collect dirty water from a stream during the dry season.

3. Campaigning for change

Oxfam is also considered a pressure group because they lobby governments and put pressure on leaders and decision-makers to bring about the change needed to end poverty and injustice across the world.

They also use the media to help them in their campaigns and to raise awareness of the needs of others.

One of Oxfam's most important campaigns has been their drive to introduce fair trade laws. They believe that current trade rules and regulations benefit richer countries while poorer countries are losing out.

For example, when poorer countries produce food and other products they often find it difficult to export them because richer countries force them to pay a high tax on the products. This prevents them from making a fair profit on the goods they are selling.

Save the Children

Save the Children was established in the UK in 1919 to improve the lives of children around the world and ensure that they had access to proper food, healthcare, education and protection. Today, Save the Children is an international charity and aid organisation that continues to improve the lives of children around the world.

▲ A representative of Save the Children at a school in Parys in Free State, South Africa, where orphaned and vulnerable children are provided with food and drink and a safe place to play.

Save the Children spends the majority of its funding (92%) where it is needed most: on the development programmes which help children and families help themselves. Save the Children also works in countries where there has been conflict or natural disasters, such as the 2010 Haiti earthquake which caused widespread devastation and destruction. It continues to campaign for children's rights and raise awareness of the needs and rights of children around the world.

Activities

3. Name **one** difficulty that countries experience as a result of conflict or natural disasters.

4. Identify and explain **one** way that NGOs like Oxfam can bring short-term relief to countries who are experiencing difficulties.

5. Explain the different ways that long-term development programmes can help countries to become more self-supporting.

War on Want

War on Want was formed in 1951 and, like Oxfam, it is a charity which highlights the needs of poverty-stricken countries across the world. It believes that it is more important to fight the root causes of poverty rather than just the effects. Similar to the other NGOs, it lobbies governments and international agencies to tackle problems and raise awareness of the issues experienced by developing countries.

War on Want believes that 'poverty is political' and that it is up to the politicians to work together to develop policies and practice that will provide an opportunity for all countries to share in global wealth. Some of its campaigns include:

■ targeting sweatshops and plantations – supporting workers to achieve their basic human rights to work in adequate conditions for fair pay

■ food justice – supporting small farmers who are being pushed out by multinational agribusiness
■ conflict zones – working with people in war zones to make sure that they can protect themselves against human rights abuses.

Activities

6. Using the Internet or library, research the work of **two** NGOs. Choose one of the campaigns they are currently involved in and explain what they are trying to achieve.

7. Evaluate the different strategies used by NGOs and pressure groups to achieve their aims. Think about how successful they are in achieving their goals and if there are any negative aspects to the methods they sometimes use to raise awareness of their campaigns. Use the information on page 29 on pressure groups to help you.

▲ A peaceful protest is one of the strategies which 'War on Want' campaigners and other NGOs use to influence decision makers to improve the lives of others.

Section 5 Key democratic institutions and their role in promoting inclusion, justice and democracy

Learning outcomes

I am learning about the features of the main institutions set up under the Good Friday Agreement, the Northern Ireland Assembly and the Executive Committee, for example:

* the Human Rights Commission
* the Police Ombudsman's Office.

This section looks at the main institutions which have been set up under the Good Friday Agreement. It examines the role of the Northern Ireland Assembly and the Executive Committee in the government of Northern Ireland, in particular the role of the Human Rights Commission and the Police Ombudsman's Office in promoting equality and justice.

What do we mean by democracy?

In Section 2 (pages 26–43) you learned that in a **democracy** everyone is given the right to vote and choose the government that they believe represents their views. In a democracy people can have a say in how the country is run and decide on issues that affect them. Other features of a democracy include:

- a multi-party system where there is more than one political party to choose from
- that the rule of law is obeyed and has the people's best interests at heart
- equality and fairness for all citizens
- people can openly criticise the government, protest and voice different opinions
- human rights are enjoyed by all citizens
- free and fair elections
- that the media is not controlled by the government
- transparency and openness in how the government is run.

The Good Friday Agreement

The current democratic government in Northern Ireland was set up after the signing of the Good Friday Agreement on 10 April 1998 by the British

▲ The government of Northern Ireland sits at Parliament Buildings on the Stormont Estate in Belfast.

and Irish governments; this is also known as the Belfast Agreement. The Agreement was a major political breakthrough for the peace process and for the people of Northern Ireland. The key issue in this Agreement was that a devolved government of Northern Ireland would be established which would be committed to power-sharing between the largest political communities. It was viewed by most people as an opportunity for Northern Ireland's divided society to resolve its differences and move forward to a future of power-sharing and equality. The majority of the electorate in both parts of Ireland endorsed it in a referendum on 22 May 1998; voters in Northern Ireland showed overwhelming support for it with 71 per cent voting 'yes'. The electorate in the Republic voted separately to change their constitution in line with the Agreement, with 94 per cent showing their support.

The Northern Ireland Assembly

The government in Northern Ireland received its powers in 1999 and now has power to make decisions on important issues which were previously made by the UK government. For this reason it is often referred to as a **'devolved government'** because the power to pass laws has been devolved (passed from) the UK government. The devolved government in Northern Ireland is called the Northern Ireland Assembly.

Having a local Assembly benefits the people of Northern Ireland because local representatives can make decisions which affect them. Local politicians usually have more understanding of the needs of the people within their part of the UK and so can make decisions which will hopefully have a positive impact on how their region is run. The Northern Ireland Assembly has responsibility for issues such as health, education, agriculture and the environment but does not have power over issues of national importance such as taxation, elections and national security; these decisions are still made by the national government in London.

Local Councils

The Northern Ireland Assembly and the UK government are not the only political institutions that make decisions which affect us. Local councils also make decisions about local issues within our communities. They are responsible for issues such as waste collection, leisure facilities, parks, organising local events and promoting their areas.

Activity

1. Who makes the decisions that affect us? Look at the statements below, decide who is responsible for dealing with each issue and then complete the table below. An example has been completed for you.

   A A decision is made to build a new recreation centre and outdoor activity area in a local park.
   B The rate of income tax is changed to increase the amount of tax people pay on their wages.
   C School holidays are set so that all schools in Northern Ireland have the same time off.
   D New targets are introduced for hospital waiting times in Northern Ireland.
   E Changes are made to raise the age that people can take part in the National Lottery to eighteen.
   F Taxes on alcohol and cigarettes are increased as a result of the Budget.
   G New cycle paths are introduced in a busy town to help reduce traffic congestion.
   H New laws are introduced to limit the number of immigrants coming into the UK.
   I Funding is increased to help farmers in Northern Ireland during the recession.
   J Planning permission is given to build a new shopping centre in the centre of a small town.

Local council	A A decision is made to build a new recreation centre and outdoor activity area in a local park.
Northern Ireland Assembly	
National (UK) Government at Westminster	

Key word
devolved government

Political landscape

Most political parties in Northern Ireland supported the Good Friday Agreement and elections to the Northern Ireland Assembly take place every four years using a system of proportional representation (see page 35).

The different political parties in Northern Ireland can be divided into three main groups:

- Nationalist/Republican, such as Sinn Fein and the Social Democratic and Labour Party (SDLP)
- non-aligned, such as the Alliance Party
- Unionist/Loyalist, such as the Democratic Unionist Party (DUP) and Ulster Unionist Party (UUP).

Activity

2. Using the Internet to help you, find out how many seats each party has in the Northern Ireland Assembly (www.niassembly.gov.uk).

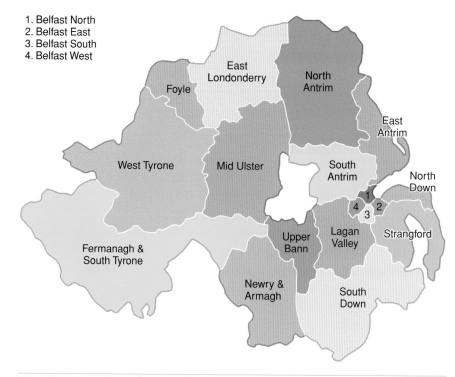

1. Belfast North
2. Belfast East
3. Belfast South
4. Belfast West

The eighteen constituencies in Northern Ireland.

Unionists identify themselves with Great Britain and are usually supported by Protestants. Nationalists identify themselves with the nation of Ireland and are usually supported by Catholics. Non-aligned parties such as the Alliance Party have a neutral standpoint and are voted for by members from all communities.

In Northern Ireland there are eighteen **constituencies** (voting areas) and from these eighteen areas, six members are chosen from different political parties; this makes a total of 108 Members of the Legislative Assembly (MLAs). MLAs are elected by the public to represent them in the Northern Ireland Assembly.

The main role of the OFMDFM and the Assembly is to legislate (pass laws) and to have a programme of government which promotes equality of opportunity for all citizens in Northern Ireland. All laws which are passed by the Assembly must be in agreement with the European Convention on Human Rights (see pages 30–31) and are monitored by the Northern Ireland Human Rights Commission (see page 56) to ensure that they are fair.

MLAs meet in the Assembly buildings at Stormont each week to discuss issues, take part in debates and vote on new laws.

The role of the Northern Ireland Assembly

The Northern Ireland Assembly is made up of the Office of the First Minister and Deputy First Minister (OFMDFM), the Executive Committee and 108 MLAs.

The Executive Committee

The **Executive Committee** is the name given to the ten departments within the Northern Ireland Assembly. Each department is run by a government Minister who is an elected member of the Assembly. They are responsible for leading and managing their department, similar to how managers in the private sector run their businesses. The ten ministerial positions are appointed fairly and are linked to how many seats the different parties have won in the Assembly elections.

Some of the departments within the Executive Committee include:

■ Department of Education

■ Department for Regional Development

■ Department of Culture, Arts and Leisure

■ Department of the Environment

■ Department of Enterprise, Trade and Investment.

Activity

3. Look at the Key words listed at the bottom of the page and match them to the following definitions:

   A A type of political system where people have their say on who will become their representatives and the laws that will be made.

   B A particular local area where the people elect MLAs to represent them.

   C Members chosen by the Assembly to be responsible for the work of the ten Northern Ireland Departments.

   D Northern Ireland has been given more control over its own affairs, in areas such as industry, education, health, agriculture, etc. This means the power to do things has moved closer to the people who are affected.

   E The idea of acting on behalf of someone else. For example, MLAs represent their constituents (the people living in the area where they were elected).

   F The ten Ministers, together with the First and Deputy First Minister form this.

   G The individuals elected to serve and represent the people of Northern Ireland in the Assembly. There are 108 of them.

Key words

constituency ■ democracy ■ devolution ■ Executive Committee ■ Ministers ■ MLAs ■ representation

Other institutions created under the Good Friday Agreement

When the Northern Ireland Assembly was set up after the signing of the Good Friday Agreement several institutions were created to promote peace and justice. Two of these are the Northern Ireland Human Rights Commission and the Police Ombudsman for Northern Ireland.

The Northern Ireland Human Rights Commission (NIHRC)

Equality and human rights were considered to be central to solving the conflict in Northern Ireland and so the creation of a human rights commission (and equality commission) was a key feature of the Good Friday Agreement. The NIHRC is *not* an NGO, nor is it a government body; it is an independent public agency whose main purpose is to promote awareness of the importance of human rights in Northern Ireland. It was the first organisation in the UK to be recognised by the United Nations as a national human rights institution.

It reviews existing law and examines proposed laws for the UK government and Northern Ireland Assembly to ensure that they are fair and in line with international human rights standards. Other work includes:

- providing resources for schools to promote human rights education
- conducting research into human rights issues
- providing training in human rights to public bodies and other organisations
- launching one of the largest consultation programmes in Northern Ireland on what should be contained in a Bill of Rights for Northern Ireland
- promoting human rights within Northern Ireland.

Issues of concern for NIHRC include: racism and the protection of ethnic minorities, sectarianism, hate crime, poverty and exclusion, and human rights within the criminal justice system.

It carries out investigations to find out if current law and practice is fair and protects the human rights of everyone within Northern Ireland.

It also offers advice and support for individuals who believe that their human rights have been abused and will assist them in bringing court proceedings if it believes that their rights have been violated.

Activities

1. Read Source A and identify and explain **one** way the migrant workers were being denied one of their human rights.

2. Identify and explain **one** way the NIHRC can protect the rights of individuals.

3. Evaluate the role of the NIHRC in helping to promote a fair and equal society in Northern Ireland.

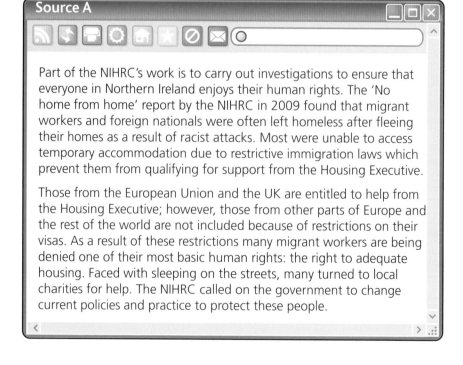

Source A

Part of the NIHRC's work is to carry out investigations to ensure that everyone in Northern Ireland enjoys their human rights. The 'No home from home' report by the NIHRC in 2009 found that migrant workers and foreign nationals were often left homeless after fleeing their homes as a result of racist attacks. Most were unable to access temporary accommodation due to restrictive immigration laws which prevent them from qualifying for support from the Housing Executive.

Those from the European Union and the UK are entitled to help from the Housing Executive; however, those from other parts of Europe and the rest of the world are not included because of restrictions on their visas. As a result of these restrictions many migrant workers are being denied one of their most basic human rights: the right to adequate housing. Faced with sleeping on the streets, many turned to local charities for help. The NIHRC called on the government to change current policies and practice to protect these people.

The Police Ombudsman for Northern Ireland

The Police Ombudsman for Northern Ireland investigates complaints made about police officers in Northern Ireland. Anyone is free to make a complaint if they feel that they have been mistreated by a police officer. It is also common procedure for the Police Ombudsman to carry out independent investigations any time that a firearm is used or baton rounds are fired.

Examples of the complaints that they deal with include:

- a member of public has accused a police officer of treating them unfairly or discriminating against them
- a police officer has been accused of breaking the law
- a police officer has not followed the code of conduct.

The Police Ombudsman is completely independent of the Police Service of Northern Ireland. This means that they carry out investigations which are impartial (not taking sides) and fair. An independent survey in 2008 showed that over 80 per cent of Catholics and Protestants believed that the Police Ombudsman was fair in how it dealt with complaints made about police officers.

The Police Ombudsman publish the results of their investigations in an annual report to ensure that the public have confidence in how they work and that they provide a fair police complaints system.

Part of their findings from their annual report (for 2009) can be seen in Source B.

Source B   Police Ombudsman's Annual Report 2009

According to the 2009 report by the Police Ombudsman's Office there were twelve police officers prosecuted and over 300 disciplined after investigations were carried out by the Police Ombudsman.

Charges of actual bodily harm, careless driving, theft and perverting the course of justice were taken against twelve PSNI officers in 2009.

Over 300 other officers were also disciplined:

- 15 faced formal proceedings for misconduct
- 23 received written warnings
- 246 were given advice and guidance from superiors
- 22 were ordered to attend management discussions.

In 2009 the Police Ombudsman's Office received a total of 3120 complaints including allegations of racial, homophobic and sectarian discrimination, and sexual assault – a rise of 3 per cent from the previous year.

However, in more than half the cases which were investigated, the Police Ombudsman's Office found no evidence to support the allegations which were made.

Activity

4. In what ways do you think the Police Ombudsman's Office promotes a fair and just society in Northern Ireland?

Section 1 Maximising and sustaining health and well-being

Learning outcomes

I am learning about:

* the contribution of diet, exercise and attitude to health and well-being

* the risks associated with alcohol, cigarette and substance abuse and other unhealthy lifestyle choices.

When most people consider their health they tend to focus on the physical state of their body and whether or not they are physically well. However, as this section will examine, being healthy is not only about physical well-being but also includes looking after ourselves both emotionally and socially. This section looks at the many ways people can look after their all-round well-being, but also the lifestyle choices that can have a negative effect on health such as drinking alcohol, smoking cigarettes, substance abuse and unhealthy eating.

Different types of health

Society is becoming increasingly health conscious. People are bombarded from sources such as **the media**, school, various health organisations, politicians and celebrities on issues relating to their health and well-being. But what does it mean to be healthy?

When we think of the term 'health', we tend to associate it with our physical well-being and whether or not we are physically ill. However, as shown in the diagram below, health encompasses a lot more:

Health has been defined by the **World Health Organisation** (WHO) as: 'A complete state of physical, mental and social well-being and not simply the absence of disease or infirmity.'

Physical health

Physical health is anything that has to do with the physical state of the body. Good physical health can help you lead a satisfying and successful life.

Emotional health

Emotional health (also known as mental health) is how you think, feel, act and how you are able to cope with life in general. To be emotionally healthy you should talk about feelings, ask for help when you need it, keep in touch with friends and do something you enjoy regularly.

Social health

Social health is concerned with how you interact with other people in various situations and how well you can make and maintain relationships. To be socially healthy you should be able to hold and contribute to conversations, have friends and to feel a sense of belonging to such groups as family, class and peers.

Health and well-being can be broken down into three parts.

Physical health

Physical health can be affected by many different factors as the table below shows.

Illness	Illnesses range from the common cold to life-threatening diseases such as cancer. Illness affects the way your body functions and affects people in different ways. Young children and the elderly are particularly susceptible to illness and, therefore, poor physical health.
Diet	Your body needs different vitamins and minerals in order to function. The body's main source of these is through food and your diet can affect the way the body works: e.g. a lack of calcium could lead to **osteoporosis**; too much salt can lead to high blood pressure and increased risk of **stroke** and coronary heart disease. The importance of a balanced diet is covered in more detail on pages 66–71.
Economic factors	How much money we have can determine what we eat. For example, processed foods which tend to be high in sugar and fat and that are produced in bulk are cheaper to buy compared to buying fresh, **organic** ingredients. Those that are less well off are more likely to buy the cheaper alternatives which over a period of time can affect physical health.
Environment	The environment can affect physical health in many ways that are generally beyond our control. There is a direct link between air quality and respiratory illnesses, such as asthma; long-term exposure to UV rays from the sun can cause skin cancer; cramped urban environments provide conditions where infections and disease can spread more easily.
Exercise	The government has provided guidelines for the amount of time people should spend exercising. There are many physical health benefits to exercising which are covered in more detail on pages 64–65.
Genes	The genetic makeup of our bodies affects our physical appearance and well-being, from eye and hair colour to height and weight. It has been scientifically proven that our genes are inherited from both parents, which means that certain diseases such as **cystic fibrosis** and **haemophilia** can be inherited.
Parents	Parents play an important role in the lives of their children. In our early lives they determine the food we eat and also influence our lifestyles and attitudes to physical health.
School	Young people spend a lot of their time in the school environment. Good physical health is encouraged in subjects such as Home Economics and PE as well as schools providing the option of healthy food at lunchtime.
Local community	The local community and surrounding areas can be beneficial or detrimental to physical health. Some local councils plan for 'green areas' and play parks for people to make use of. However, some local communities have very little to do and as a result young people can turn to alcohol and **drugs** out of boredom.

Table displaying the factors affecting physical health.

Activities

1. Look at the factors that affect physical health in the table above. In groups, rank them in order of how much you think they affect your physical health, with 1 being the most influential and 9 being the least. Give **three** reasons for your number 1 choice and explain your decision.

2. Imagine you had a serious physical illness. Identify and explain how this would affect:

   a) your family

   b) your friends

   c) your school work.

Key words

cystic fibrosis ▪ drugs ▪ haemophilia ▪ the media ▪ organic ▪ osteoporosis ▪ stroke ▪ The World Health Organisation (WHO)

Social health

In 1947, the WHO stated that how a person interacts with people and society affects their overall well-being. Studies have shown that those who interact well with society tend to lead longer and more fulfilling lives and that those who are isolated tend to be more at risk of illness.

There are many ways to improve social health. These include:

- talking to family and peers often

- actively listening to people and responding to what they have to say

- developing conversational skills

- having positive body language

- learning to accept constructive criticism

- treating others in the way you would like to be treated

- engaging in a new social situation to meet new people

- trying to be positive when talking with people.

▲ Factors that can improve social health.

However, there are many ways that social health could be threatened. People's social health may be at risk if:

- they are being bullied or feel threatened

- they have low self-esteem and self-confidence

- they do not practise their social skills often – for example, they may spend most of their time in front of the computer

- family pressure or commitments do not allow for much socialising – for example, caring for a sick relative.

▲ Factors that can have a negative impact on social health.

Activity

3. How can social health be affected by different factors? Copy and complete the table.

Factor	Positively affect	Negatively affect
Housing		People are sometimes embarrassed about where they live or the type of accommodation they live in; therefore, they might not ask people around, making socialising difficult.
Environment		
School		
Workplace	• Allows interaction with other people. • Allows you to develop good communication skills.	
Computer/Internet		

Emotional health

Emotional well-being (also known as mental well-being) is considered to be just as important as our physical well-being. It is concerned with how we think, how we feel and how we control our emotions.

Emotional health problems can affect anyone at any age and take many different forms which include **depression**, **eating disorders**, **addictions**, anxiety and confusion. In general, emotional health problems in young people are caused by a combination of stresses and pressures which can include the following:

Loss of friendship: a loss of a friend will leave a gap in someone's life which can lead to depression or anxiety.

Parental difficulties: family arguments, separation and divorce are a few of the common issues young people have to deal with. Young people may become stressed, confused or feel vulnerable.

FACTORS THAT CAN AFFECT EMOTIONAL HEALTH

Bereavement: the BBC estimates that about 180,000 children under the age of sixteen lose a parent every year in the UK. Adapting to such a life-changing event can take many years. Anger, denial, guilt, fear of the unknown, depression and anxiety are just some of the many emotions a bereaved person may feel.

Loss of job: losing a job can generate feelings of uselessness, inadequacy, shame and anger. As a result of losing a job, a person may develop money worries which can contribute to stress.

Moving school or house: any big change can be particularly stressful for all involved. Losing contact with friends and familiar surroundings may cause feelings of anxiousness, loneliness and, in extreme cases, can result in depression and suicidal feelings.

Factors that can negatively affect emotional health.

Emotional health problems can also be caused by: physical factors such as illness, drug misuse or dementia; environmental factors such as poor living or work environment; and social causes such as feeling under pressure to succeed.

There are many ways in which people can seek help for emotional health problems. Actively talking about their problems, visiting their GP, counselling, psychotherapy, complementary therapies and taking medication can all help overcome problems.

Emotional health can also be improved by:

- **Changing jobs:** starting fresh in a new job can give both feelings of accomplishment and self-worth as well as the sense of leaving old stresses behind.

- **Forming a new friendship:** having someone new to talk to and share feelings with can lessen the burden of stress.
- **Joining a club or society:** can create a sense of belonging and purpose. It allows a person to be more sociable and may take their mind off any problems that they have.
- **Taking up a new hobby or interest:** allows the person to meet new people, exercise their body and mind and can also increase **self-esteem**.
- **Developing a new skill:** can allow the person to feel a sense of achievement and give someone a more positive outlook on life.

Other ways to maintain good emotional health include being physically active, maintaining a balanced diet, having a healthy work/life balance and sleeping well.

Source A

This poster from the Mental Health Foundation shows ten ways in which you can look after your mental health.

talk about your feelings   keep active   eat well   drink sensibly   keep in touch with friends and loved ones

ask for help   take a break   do something you're good at   accept who you are   care for others

Ways to look after your mental health
www.mentalhealth.org.uk

Mental **Health** Foundation

Activities

4. Study Source A. Explain how each of the ten diagrams shown could contribute to better emotional health.

5. You have been asked to help with the design of a new school. The principal wants to maximise the health of all pupils – physically, emotionally and socially. List **six** pieces of advice you would give the principal about the layout and facilities the new school should have, taking into consideration all the different types of health.

Key words

addiction ▪ bereavement ▪ depression ▪ eating disorder ▪ self-esteem

Exercise

Exercise has many proven physical, emotional and social health benefits and can be defined as an activity or an effort whereby people aim to improve physical fitness and overall health.

Exercise and physical health

Keeping physically active can prevent major illnesses and is the basis for a healthier lifestyle. The UK government recommends that adults aim to do at least 30 minutes of moderate intensity activity on five or more days per week and that children and young people do around 60 minutes every day.

BUPA states that the signs that you're doing moderate intensity activity are:

■ *an increase in your breathing rate*
■ *an increase in your heart rate to a point where you can feel your pulse*
■ *feeling warm.*

Physical activity does not necessarily mean everyone should take time out to go to the gym for long periods of time, but instead it can be incorporated into everyday life – for example, walking to and from school, cycling, taking the stairs instead of a lift.

There are many physical health benefits of doing exercise; some are short-term, others are more likely to benefit you in the long-term. These are shown in the diagram at the bottom of the page.

Apart from the many physical benefits exercise can bring, exercise has been known to help improve emotional and social health. Physical activity helps get rid of stress and aggression in a harmless way. Success in physical activity or sport can improve self-confidence and self-esteem. Additionally, it can give you something to aim for, provide a challenge and increase motivation. Studies have shown that people who exercise tend to be more optimistic and happy compared to those who do not.

In addition, social health can be improved by leading an active life. Exercising helps you meet new people and make friends especially if you join a sports team, gym or exercise class which can help you learn and develop new skills – for example, teamwork and co-operation – as well as giving you a sense of belonging.

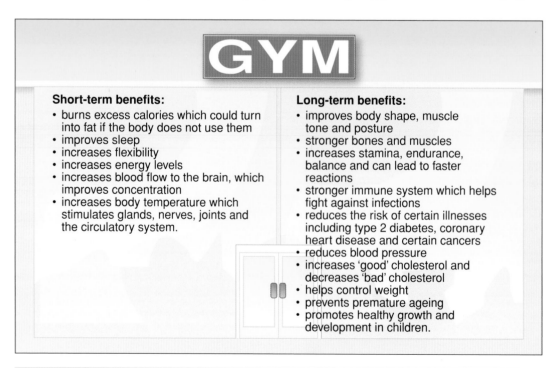

Short-term benefits:
• burns excess calories which could turn into fat if the body does not use them
• improves sleep
• increases flexibility
• increases energy levels
• increases blood flow to the brain, which improves concentration
• increases body temperature which stimulates glands, nerves, joints and the circulatory system.

Long-term benefits:
• improves body shape, muscle tone and posture
• stronger bones and muscles
• increases stamina, endurance, balance and can lead to faster reactions
• stronger immune system which helps fight against infections
• reduces the risk of certain illnesses including type 2 diabetes, coronary heart disease and certain cancers
• reduces blood pressure
• increases 'good' cholesterol and decreases 'bad' cholesterol
• helps control weight
• prevents premature ageing
• promotes healthy growth and development in children.

The short-term and long-term benefits of doing exercise.

Source A   Change4Life poster

Source B   Female bodybuilder

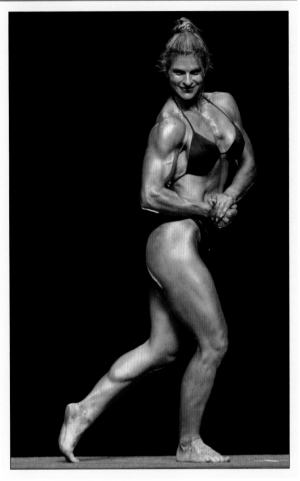

Activities

1. Identify and explain ways you could become more physically active by changing certain elements of your daily routine.

2. Having clear goals can help motivate you and keep you focused. Identify your top **three** fitness goals for the next month.

3. What do you think the key message in Source A is? Is this the best way to deliver the message?

4. Do you think the poster in Source A and its message could affect young people's exercising habits? Identify and explain **three** reasons for your answer.

5. Look at Source B. Do you think over-exercising can be a negative thing? Identify and explain **two** reasons for your answer.

Key word
exercise

A balanced diet

Eating the right foods and consuming the correct nutrients in the right quantities is an important step towards good health. Studies have shown that the more balanced and nutritious a person's diet, the healthier they will be. What we eat affects our mood, growth and ability to concentrate. The National Health Service **(NHS)** recommends that people should eat from the five main food groups. These are:

- bread, cereal (including breakfast cereals) and potatoes (starchy foods)
- fruit (including fresh fruit juice) and vegetables
- meat and fish
- milk and dairy foods
- fat and sugar.

From looking at Source A (below) it is clear that we should eat plenty of fruit and vegetables and starchy foods but limit foods which are high in fat and sugar.

Part of a balanced diet also includes eating at regular times. It is recommended that we eat three main meals per day – breakfast, lunch and dinner.

Importance of a balanced diet

A balanced diet provides the following benefits:

- **Physical health:** if a person eats a balanced diet, their **immune system** will be stronger which will help prevent and fight infections. Studies have also shown that, by eating correctly, the risk of certain types of cancers decreases and blood pressure may be lower.
- **Controlling weight:** eating a balanced diet and monitoring portion sizes will lead to an improved control over weight. It will also provide the body with more energy, enabling a person to exercise without getting tired easily.
- **Healthy body growth:** a balanced diet will provide essential nutrients for muscle, tissue and bone growth and should be started early in life so it can become a routine as opposed to something people struggle to maintain.
- **Healthy mind:** a balanced diet is also beneficial to emotional health. It can help you to make decisions and tackle problems and memory may also improve.

The diets of most young people are influenced by what is available at home and at school. In 2006, celebrity chef Jamie Oliver campaigned to improve the diet of schoolchildren across the UK by attempting to change the school meals system by banning **junk food** and introducing more fresh food to school lunchtime menus.

Source A   The recommended allowance of foods as suggested by eatwell.gov.uk

◀ Jamie Oliver campaigning for improved school meals across the UK.

School meals were such an important issue that Jamie Oliver wrote a manifesto to help persuade the UK Government to take action. Jamie set out proposals for schools, teachers, parents and dinner staff to not only re-educate people about their own eating habits but also to make fundamental changes to the foods available for young people.

Jamie made the following proposals:

For schools: make life skills and cooking classes compulsory for young people so that they are aware of good eating habits from a young age and have the necessary skills to cook for themselves.

For teachers: ensure non-core subjects such as cookery and life skills are not overlooked so that young people's right to cookery lessons is adequately met.

For principals: ensure that school meals are based on nutritional content and not just cost and to make schools into junk food-free areas.

For parents: ensure that all parents understand their role in terms of providing the correct nutrients and foods for their children at home.

For dinner staff: ensure dinner staff have the necessary skills, tools and ingredients to provide school meals that are interesting, tasty and have nutritional value.

Activity

1. With reference to the text above relating to Jamie Oliver's campaign for better school meals and your own knowledge, evaluate how practical his ideas are.

Key words

immune system ▪ junk food ▪ NHS

Difficulties of a balanced diet

People can often find it difficult to stick to a balanced diet. They tend to lead busy lives and so find it difficult to prepare fresh meals and some cannot help giving in to the temptation of unhealthy foods.

The availability of junk food, convenience food and fast food makes it easy for people to disregard the benefits of a balanced diet. This topic discusses what each of these types of food are and why they are popular.

Junk food

The term 'junk food' is generally used to describe food that is low in nutritional value and high in **calories**. Based on this, it should never form the foundation of anyone's diet. People are often attracted to this type of food for many reasons, as shown in the diagram on page 69. Some examples of junk food include: sweets, crisps, fizzy drinks, burgers and pizza.

Advertising junk food

Young people are constantly bombarded with junk food advertisements. According to the Food Standards Agency, junk food advertising directly influences children's food preferences. It therefore undermines the messages about healthy eating young people receive.

Channel 4 estimates that, on television alone, £480 million is spent each year advertising products high in fat, salt and sugar and, although junk food adverts are currently banned during children's television programmes, it is estimated that 70 per cent of children watch most television between the hours of 6p.m. and 9p.m. Based on this, there has been a call from the Children's Food Campaign to completely ban all junk food adverts before the watershed (9p.m.).

Convenience food

The term 'convenience food' is generally used to describe food which is processed and is designed for quick and easy consumption. It is usually pre-prepared, ready to eat or involves only heating. Typical convenience foods include: microwaveable meals, TV dinners, pre-cooked rice, noodle pots, soup sachets and luncheon meats.

▲ Microwaveable meals are classed as convenience foods and tend to be high in calories and low in nutritional value.

One of the main reasons people may choose these types of food is that they do not have enough time to prepare fresh meals from scratch due to busy work and family schedules.

Fast food

Fast food generally refers to food that is prepared and served quickly. It is typically cheap to buy and is usually bought from a restaurant or takeaway, for example McDonalds.

Fast food tends to be criticised due to its low nutritional value and includes such foods as fish and chips, pizza, burgers, fried chicken and kebabs. The popularity of fast food can be seen from the worldwide success of restaurant chains such as Burger King and KFC.

▲ Fast food is widely available and has been heavily criticised in the past.

Why do people choose to eat such foods?

There are many reasons why people choose to eat fast food, convenience food and junk food and many reasons why they shouldn't as illustrated in the diagram below:

Useful weblinks

www.caloriecounting.co.uk

www.caloriecount.about.com

www.weightlossresources.co.uk

Why people choose to eat fast food/junk food/convenience food	Why people shouldn't eat fast food/junk food/convenience food
• taste • low cost • readily available • extensive advertising • quick or no preparation time • can be part of a social event.	• low nutritional value • can be addictive • unknown food content • desire to lose weight • desire to eat a balanced diet • desire to learn how to cook.

Key word

calories

Activities

2. Do you think that packaging on junk food encourages young people to buy it? Identify and explain **two** reasons for your answer.

3. **a)** Research the nutritional value of the foods in the table below. This can be done by looking at the packaging or using a company's website for nutritional information.

   b) Does any of the information you gathered surprise you?

c) Now that you know the nutritional information of some popular junk food, would it make you think twice about eating it? Why?

4. Identify all the junk food you have consumed this week. Do you feel this is part of a balanced diet? Explain your answer.

5. Evaluate the role of fast food in today's society.

	Salt	Fats (saturated)	Calories
Big Mac			
Large portion of French fries			
Medium-sized pizza			
Mars Bar			
Packet of crisps			
Tub of Pringles			
A Pot Noodle			

Health risks of an unhealthy diet

There are many health risks of an unbalanced diet. If the body lacks a particular vitamin or mineral it can lead to a **deficiency**-related disease. For example, a lack of vitamin C can cause scurvy, a lack of calcium can result in brittle bones and the lack of iron can result in **anaemia**. Similarly, if the body receives too much of certain vitamins and minerals it will not function to the best of its ability.

Perhaps the biggest food-related health risk to people in Northern Ireland is an unbalanced diet where people take in too much salt, sugar and fat. The table below shows the main health risks which can occur as a result of excess amounts of each of these food types:

Nutrient	Excess amounts can cause:
Salt	High blood pressure; coronary heart disease; a stroke
Sugar	Tooth decay; weight gain or **obesity**; an aggravation of asthma; mood swings
Fat	High blood cholesterol which can cause heart disease; weight gain or obesity

Obesity

Obesity is the term used to describe a person who is 20 per cent over the recommended weight for their build and height according to the Body Mass Index (BMI). Obesity develops gradually from a combination of factors as shown in the diagram at the bottom of the page.

Obesity is a huge problem in Northern Ireland. On 16 March 2010, Chief Medical Officer Michael McBride said that as many as one in four people are obese in Northern Ireland. He said that one in five boys and one in four girls in primary one are considered to be overweight or obese, indicating that obesity will be a problem for the foreseeable future.

Methods for tackling obesity

In order to try to lose weight, some people opt for 'quick fix' invasive procedures; for example, having a gastric band or balloon fitted. There are also many 'crash' diets which may help but these can be difficult to stick to and maintain weight loss. In extreme cases a doctor can prescribe weight loss medication, but only to those who can show that they can't lose weight when following a calorie-controlled diet.

Arguably the best way of tackling obesity is to make a long-term commitment to reduce the intake of calories and exercise more. Many people have found that joining a self-help group or a weight loss organisation can offer support. Additional advice and help is available from medical professionals such as GPs and dieticians who can monitor weight loss and offer exercise plans and help with diets.

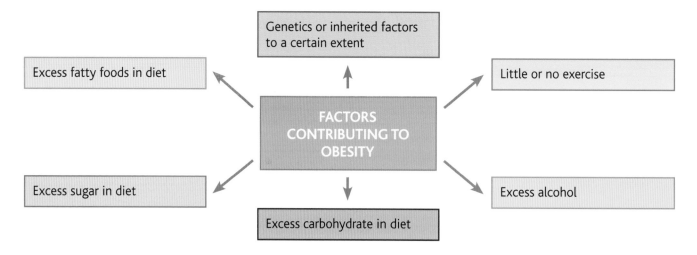

Risks associated with obesity

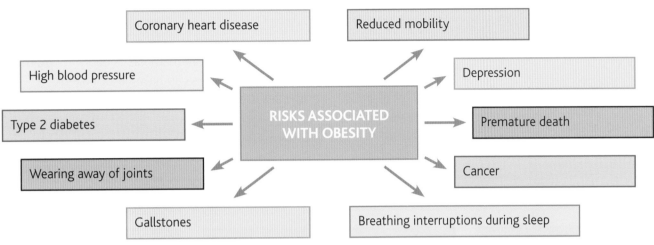

Coronary heart disease

Reduced mobility

High blood pressure

Depression

Type 2 diabetes

RISKS ASSOCIATED WITH OBESITY

Premature death

Wearing away of joints

Cancer

Gallstones

Breathing interruptions during sleep

Source C (*Belfast Telegraph* article on obesity, November 2009)

Obesity timebomb 'could bring down Northern Ireland's health service'

Two-thirds of men and 50 per cent of women across Northern Ireland are expected to be clinically obese by 2050, leading to the collapse of the health service, assembly members have warned.

The Stormont Health Committee has proposed a series of recommendations to tackle the growing problem of obesity in Northern Ireland – including compulsory PE classes for all schoolchildren, restrictions on advertising foods with high levels of salt, sugar and fat, and the traffic light labelling system becoming the norm on all food sold across the province.

In September Northern Ireland's Chief Medical Officer Michael McBride revealed that the impact of obesity causes around 450 deaths every year and reduces life expectancy by up to nine years.

Belfast Telegraph (www.belfasttelegraph.co.uk)

Activities

6. Read Source C and answer the following questions.

   a) Why might assembly members think that the health service may collapse?

   b) Do you think that banning food advertisements will affect the obesity levels in Northern Ireland?

   c) What is meant by 'traffic light labelling system'? You may want to use the Food Standards Agency website to help you.

7. Some schools have considered sending letters home to parents if their child is overweight. Evaluate how effective you think this initiative would be.

Key words

anaemia ▪ deficiency ▪ obesity

Drugs

A drug is any substance that affects the way the body or mind works. When we think of drugs we tend to think of illegal substances such as cannabis or cocaine. However, many drugs are legal in the eyes of the law but can still be dangerous – for example, alcohol. In addition, millions of pounds are spent every year to develop drugs to be used for medical purposes.

Drugs can usually be classified into four main areas as shown below. There are times, however, where certain drugs can fall into more than one category: for example high strength cannabis can have hallucinogenic properties as well as being a depressant.

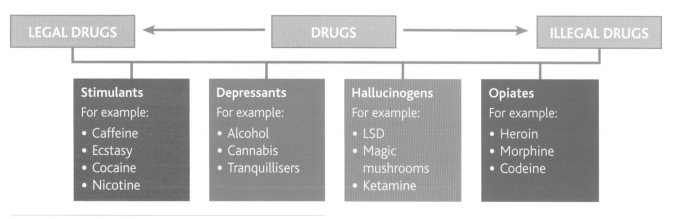

Four main categories of drugs.

Stimulants

Stimulants speed up the **central nervous system** and speed up brain activity. They often make you feel more alert, lively, talkative, confident and **euphoric**. They postpone the feelings of tiredness and, therefore, they are popular among partygoers and clubbers. When the effects start to wear off, people may become tired, irritable, have mood swings and become restless. These feelings could often tempt people into taking the drug again and so beginning a cycle of drug taking.

Depressants

Depressants are often prescribed by the doctor as they help reduce feelings of anxiety, panic and stress. They make a person calmer and can help induce sleep by slowing down the central nervous system and brain activity. However, depressants can be abused and side effects can include clumsiness, dizziness, slurred speech and confusion. In severe cases they have been known to cause loss of consciousness and even death.

Hallucinogens

Hallucinogens are substances that affect the senses and alter the drug user's perception. People taking hallucinogenic drugs may see, feel or hear things that in reality are not there and may have little or no concept of speed or distance. Hallucinations can have an effect on the user's mood – for example, if they have a 'bad trip' it could be terrifying and terrorise their thoughts. Short-term side effects include increased blood pressure, increased heart rate, memory loss and itching. Long-term side effects could include flashbacks, impaired thinking, outbursts of violence and mood swings.

Opiates

Opiates come from the poppy plant. They are a very powerful drug that can be prescribed by the doctor for pain relief – for example, morphine. However, if opiates are abused – for example, using heroin – there can be many side effects. These include: feelings of euphoria, dry mouth, vomiting, weak muscles, decreased appetite and thirst, a reduction in heart rate and brain activity and a reduction in breathing rate. Over time, the body can become tolerant of and dependent on the drug and require more to achieve desired results.

Why do young people experiment with drugs?

Young people are attracted to drug taking for a variety of reasons as shown in the diagram below:

Source A An extract taken from a leading UK website for teachers and education professionals

Jim Weir of the Forum for Action on Substance Abuse (FASA) said that drugs charities were concerned about substance misuse in young children. 'Last year we started to work with pupils in P5 (aged nine to ten) after we became aware that 11-year-olds were using drugs,' he said. 'We want to get in there before they get to the age where they are beginning to use.'

The *Times Educational Supplement*

Peer pressure: a lot of young people start taking drugs because people in their peer group are taking them and there is a pressure to fit in with everyone else.

Stress: young people can become stressed for many reasons including school, parents and **bullying**. Some may want to escape their stressful situations and may experiment with drugs to make them feel good.

Availability: many young people know where to get illegal drugs if they want them. This can make it difficult to say no. Legal drugs – for example, alcohol and nicotine – are also very accessible.

Curiosity: most young people are naturally curious. Drugs are an issue that is often talked about in school and this can lead to a desire to experiment.

WHY YOUNG PEOPLE EXPERIMENT WITH DRUGS

Pleasure: this is one of the strongest influences on young people. If a young person is under the impression that a drug makes them 'feel good', they are going to be inclined to take it.

Lifestyle: there are situations where drugs are considered to be more acceptable. For example, many young people experiment with drugs in night clubs. In some areas where there is high unemployment and low wages, drug use also increases.

Low cost: drugs can be cheaper than alcohol and the effects may last longer, so young people may see drugs as value for money.

Rebellion: young people have been told over and over by parents, school and charities how drugs are bad for them. Risk taking is a normal part of growing up and young people have a tendency to rebel during their teenage years.

Why young people choose to experiment with drugs.

Activities

1. On your own, place the reasons why young people experiment with drugs in the diagram above in order of importance, with 1 being the most likely cause. Identify and explain **three** reasons for your answer.

2. Read Source A. Do you agree that drug charities should work with nine- to ten-year-olds? Identify and explain **two** reasons for your answer.

3. With reference to Source A and your own knowledge, evaluate the impact drug charities could have when talking to children as young as nine.

Key words

bullying ▪ central nervous system ▪ depressants ▪ euphoric ▪ hallucinogens ▪ opiates ▪ peer pressure ▪ stimulant

Effects of commonly used drugs

There are many reasons why young people should not take drugs as they have many negative effects on the body and mind. However, it can also be argued that some drugs (which are usually legal) can have a positive effect. The tables on these pages show that the majority of drugs tend to have more negative than positive effects.

Paracetamol: Paracetamol can be bought over the counter in pharmacies and shops. It is generally used as a pain killer.

What are the effects?	
• Reduces pain • Can reduce body temperature	• Overdoses can be fatal • Liver damage after prolonged use • Other side effects are rare but can include: skin rashes; blood disorders; swollen pancreas; diarrhoea; vomiting

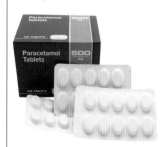

Alcohol: Alcohol is created when grains, vegetables or fruit are fermented. It comes in various brands, types and strengths and is legal to purchase when you are eighteen or over.

What are the effects?	
• Can make you feel more relaxed • Can make you feel more confident	• Is a depressant • Can be addictive • Lowers inhibitions • Slows reactions • Affects co-ordination • Can cause: slurred speech; nausea; alcohol poisoning; dehydration; loss of consciousness; infertility; obesity; brain damage; liver damage

Coffee/Tea: Coffee and tea contain caffeine. Caffeine is a natural stimulant which is found in many foods and beverages.

What are the effects?	
• Reduces tiredness • Increases alertness • Contains antioxidants which are good for the heart	• Leads to **dependency** • Can cause: restlessness; nausea; sleep difficulties; increased urine production causing dehydration; irregular heartbeats; increased blood pressure

Cigarettes: The main addictive drug in cigarettes is nicotine. Studies have shown that nicotine is harder to give up than heroin. It causes changes in the brain and makes people want to use it more and more.

What are the effects?	
• Increases alertness • Can help relaxation	• Highly addictive • Expensive • Can cause: lung cancer; throat cancer; loss of smell and taste; reduced fertility; gangrene; respiratory illnesses; gum disease; high blood pressure; premature ageing

Cannabis: Cannabis is a natural substance from the cannabis (or marijuana) plant. Cannabis is also known as: marijuana, draw, dope, puff, hash, pot, spliff, wacky backy or weed. It is an illegal substance which can be eaten, smoked or inhaled.

What are the effects?	
• Can make you feel sociable • Can make you feel relaxed • Gives pain relief	• Affects short-term memory • Brings on food cravings • Can cause: paranoia; lack of energy; negative mood changes; anxiety; depression • When smoked with tobacco can cause cancer and heart disease

Solvents: Solvent abuse involves inhaling the fumes from household or industrial products such as deodorants or glue.

What are the effects?	
• Feelings of euphoria can be experienced 	• Instant death • Hallucinations • Disorientation • Unpredictable behaviour • Blurred vision • Black-outs • Slurred speech • Heart, liver and kidney damage • Brain damage

Ecstasy: Ecstasy is an illegal drug which is a stimulant with hallucinogenic properties. It is often referred to as an 'E' or 'XTC'. It is usually taken orally in tablet or capsule form.

What are the effects?	
• Will feel alert and energetic • Feelings of euphoria can be experienced 	• Interferes with the body's ability to control temperature and dehydration • Prevents the body getting rid of water • Increases breathing rate and heart rate • Emotions are more intense • Can cause: increased blood pressure; sleep problems; mental illness; mood swings; liver and kidney problems; blood clots; psychological dependence

Mushrooms: Sometimes called 'magic mushrooms' and are naturally occurring in the wild but can also be harvested. There are two main types but both have similar effects to LSD or Acid where a user can experience a 'good trip' or a 'bad trip'.

What are the effects?	
• May make you feel euphoric, confident and relaxed 	• Can cause: hallucinations; colour and shape distortions; nausea; diarrhoea; dizziness; paranoia; flashbacks; accidental death or **suicide**; psychological dependence • Tolerance quickly develops

Source B — The Misuse of Drugs Act – Maximum penalties (October 2010)

Class	Maximum Penalty for possession (having them)	Maximum Penalty for supplying (selling or giving them away)
A	Up to seven years in prison or an unlimited fine, or both.	Up to life in prison or an unlimited fine, or both.
B	Up to five years in prison or an unlimited fine, or both.	Up to fourteen years in prison or an unlimited fine, or both.
C	Up to two years in prison or an unlimited fine, or both.	Up to fourteen years in prison or an unlimited fine, or both.

Activities

4. Look at Source B. In the past few years the government has changed cannabis from a class 'B' drug, to a class 'C' drug and then back to a class 'B' drug. Which class do you think cannabis should be in? Identify and explain **three** reasons for your answer.

5. There is a debate that the legal age of drinking alcohol should be raised to 21 from eighteen as in America. Do you think if this was brought in as a law in Northern Ireland it would have any effect on young people drinking? Why? Identify and explain **three** reasons for your answer.

6. Legal drugs like paracetamol can be bought in places like supermarkets and petrol stations. Evaluate the accessibility of this drug.

Key words

dependency ■ suicide

Consequences of experimenting with drugs

There are many negative health effects of taking drugs, some of which have been covered on pages 74–75. However, experimenting with drugs also can have a negative effect on other aspects of young people's lives and can influence those around them. This is discussed in more detail in this topic.

School

Taking drugs can greatly affect young people who attend school. Drugs can affect the body and mind. If the mind is impaired by substance abuse it is not going to perform the way it should which will affect learning and school work.

When taking drugs, a person may feel less responsibility and consequently be more prone to skip class, miss deadlines and may not care if grades start to fall. Taking drugs can also interrupt sleeping patterns which, combined with side effects, may cause a drug user to

▲ Drugs can affect school attendance.

become irritable and act out of character which could cause problems with teachers.

A person may also pick up a reputation as a drug user. Reputations like this are hard to shake off, even if the person stops using drugs.

Family

The closest people to a young person are usually in their family and they know their habits and personality well. Drugs can cause changes – for example a change in friends, a change in health or a change in personality. If a person changes, family members may become suspicious of such behaviour.

Parents may go through a range of emotions after finding out – for example, panic, confusion, anger, bewilderment and guilt. Relationships could break down during such times and drug taking can create a lot of worries for families. Many parents of drug abusers have said that their own health has suffered after finding out about their child's drug use, due to the stress and pressure this can bring.

Siblings are also affected by drug taking in the family. It is not unusual for the relationships between brothers and sisters to break down. The child with the drug problem often takes centre stage and consequently the other children in the household may feel neglected. Furthermore, there is also the possibility that siblings could follow in the footsteps of the drug user and try drugs for themselves.

▲ Drugs can affect everyone in a family.

Friends

Friends can have a negative or positive effect when it comes to taking drugs. Peer pressure, especially from friends, can lead to experimentation with drugs. However, in circumstances where one person in a circle of friends is taking drugs and the others are not, relationships can be strained.

Drug users can become withdrawn from the group, often preferring to spend time alone or socialising with other drug users. Drug users can also be prone to dramatic mood swings whereby they are happy one minute but depressed the next; this may be difficult for their friends to handle. Friendships can be further tested if drug users lie and refuse to see that they have a problem.

Despite this, if or when a person realises they have a serious problem, they may require the support of their friends to help them recover.

▲ Drugs can affect friendships.

Society

People have become accustomed to the fact that drugs exist and the common consensus is that they are bad not only for the individual, their family and friends but also for society as a whole.

Drug addiction can lead to people committing crimes in order to get money to feed their habit. As crime increases so too does the cost required to deal with it. More police resources are used and prisons fill up.

Drugs and related illness cost the NHS millions each year. These costs include **rehabilitation** for addicts, dealing with diseases caused by drug use, dealing with overdoses and dealing with accidents that occur when someone is drunk or on drugs.

Drug users also affect the local economy. **Absenteeism** from work through drug use affects businesses.

▲ Drug users may turn to crime to fund their addiction.

Additionally, drug users often can find it difficult or are unwilling to find employment. High rates of unemployment lead to increased numbers of people claiming benefits and this puts further strain on tax payers and the government.

Source C　Statistics

This chart is based on statistics from the Northern Ireland Drug Addicts Index 2009. It shows the number of registered addicts to controlled drugs such as cocaine, morphine and heroin.

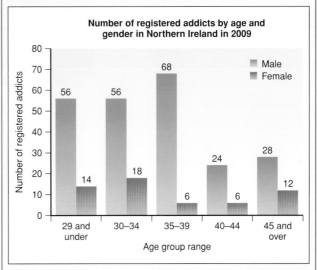

Number of registered addicts by age and gender in Northern Ireland in 2009

Age group range	Male	Female
29 and under	56	14
30–34	56	18
35–39	68	6
40–44	24	6
45 and over	28	12

Activities

7. Explain **three** ways drug taking could affect a drug user's boyfriend/girlfriend.

8. If you found out your boyfriend/girlfriend was a drug addict, what would you do?

9. Look at Source C.

   a) Explain why you think more men are registered drug addicts.

   b) Explain why you think the age groups 30–34 and 35–39 show the highest incidence of drug use.

Key words

absenteeism ■ rehabilitation ■ siblings

Helping those with a drug problem

Drug experimentation often leads to addiction and dependency, and drug addicts usually require help to give up. There are many sources of help available but generally the first step is the drug user admitting that they have a problem. This topic looks at the different options available to a person recovering from drug use and addiction.

Health professionals

The first step in recovering from drug or alcohol addiction is generally visiting your GP. GPs will ask questions such as what drugs are taken and how frequently they are taken in order to ascertain the best course of action and what type of treatment may be required.

In severe cases a person may have to be hospitalised, particularly if they experience **withdrawal symptoms** such as headaches, irregular heart palpitations, seizures or hallucinations.

Counselling/Therapy

Regular counselling can help overcome the psychological dependency of drugs. Counselling can help people explore what led to addiction and how to deal with those issues without the need for drugs. Counselling is considered an important step in preventing **relapses** back into addiction and can help people move on with their lives.

Therapy is similar to counselling but can include group discussions about life choices and current issues people within the group are having.

Rehabilitation

Rehabilitation or 'rehab' is perhaps the most widely known treatment for drug addiction. Private clinics such as The Priory have become recognisable for the work they do in helping celebrities fight drug addiction. Rehab is also available through the NHS and generally involves addicts staying on site for several weeks.

▲ Group therapy is one of the options available in recovering from drug misuse.

Residents usually take part in group therapy, one-to-one counselling and activities such as life skills, art therapy, cooking classes, money management and sport.

Schools

Schools adopt a zero tolerance policy towards drugs and integrate drug education into the curriculum. They often take part in anti-drug initiatives and invite guest speakers to advise young people to stay away from drugs.

Schools usually provide a great support network, where if you feel that you want to talk to someone about a problem, they can help. Schools often link up with youth workers and councillors who can offer help, advice and guidance about giving up drugs.

The media

As will be examined on page 88, the media strongly affects youth culture and can be used to raise awareness and highlight important issues.

At times the media is used as a tool for preventing drug use, by warning teenagers and their parents of the effects of drugs – for example, the poster campaign launched by the Health Education Authority in 1996 (see the image on page 79). At times it is used to try to shock people out of using drugs by using powerful images.

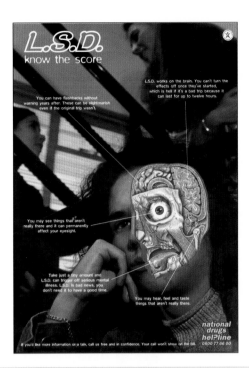

▲ A poster launched by the Health Education Authority in 1996.

Sometimes the media takes a negative stance on celebrities who abuse drugs and many stories and pictures have been published about the topic. For example, prior to her death in 2011, there were numerous negative headlines about the singer-songwriter Amy Winehouse's drug use. Look at an example headline taken from the *Daily Mail* below:

The night Amy Winehouse almost died in my arms of a drug overdose

The negative media portrayal of Amy Winehouse and other celebrities, such as the supermodel Kate Moss, has put many young people off experimenting with drugs and could help encourage those on drugs to give up.

The media is a very useful tool if targeted properly. Campaigns that draw attention to charities or booklets and posters that help young people have had success in the past. One of the biggest success stories is *Talk to Frank* where TV advertisements were used to highlight the support and advice available to young people on their website.

Self-help groups

Self-help groups can offer a support network to drug users. People may find it easier to give up their addiction if they have the help and support of others going through similar problems. There are lots self-help groups available, many of which are locally organised and funded. Some examples of self-help groups include Alcoholics Anonymous and Narcotics Anonymous.

Charities

Drug addiction charities such as Northern Ireland's Alcohol and Drug Treatment charity – the **Northern Ireland Community Addiction Service (NICAS)** – offers services such as counselling and treatment on an individual basis similar to the NHS. They can also provide help and financial support for family and friends when someone close to them has a problem.

The law and addiction

Drug addiction can lead to people committing crime in order to feed their habit. The **criminal justice system** in the UK imposes serious sentences on those caught in possession of drugs – for example, up to seven years in prison for possession and life imprisonment for those making or selling class A drugs. However, it is argued that sentencing people to time in prison is not the best solution to dealing with drug-related crime. Those who commit crime to fund a drug habit may be criminals in the eyes of the law but they also require specialised help in order to deal with their addiction. As such all prisoners in the UK can follow special rehab programmes while in prison in order to help them.

Activities

10. How could your local community help someone with a drug problem? Identify and explain **three** possible ways.

11. Take each of the subtitles above (**Health professionals, Charities, etc.**) and give **one** reason why the strategy may not work for someone dependent on drugs.

12. Evaluate the decision to send a drug addict who has committed a crime to prison.

13. Go to the NICAS website (www.nicas.info). Identify the services this charity offers.

Key words

Criminal Justice System ■ Northern Ireland Community Addiction Service (NICAS) ■ relapse ■ withdrawal symptoms

Why do young people smoke and drink?

Young people today choose to experiment with drinking alcohol and smoking cigarettes despite restrictions on sales and numerous campaigns to intervene. This topic looks at the reasons behind what influences young people to take up drinking or smoking.

Alcohol

Alcohol is widely used among teenagers.

A report put together by the Church of Ireland estimates that about 80 per cent of young people have consumed alcohol before the age of sixteen in Northern Ireland.

Young people are aware of the many health risks associated with alcohol (see pages 72–74). They learn about it in school, they are bombarded with media messages telling them that alcohol is bad and parents or carers usually warn against the dangers. However, the question remains: if these health risks are so widely known, why is alcohol still so widely used by young people? A few reasons why they might take up drinking are shown in the diagram on the right.

Availability: alcohol is widely available. Some shops, pubs and off licences are still not as strict as they should be when it comes to asking for ID so it can be easy for a minor to get their hands on alcohol. People who are legally allowed to buy alcohol have been known to purchase alcohol for younger people.

Packaging: to date, alcohol packaging does not carry any health warnings and young people tend not to stop and think about the dangers of alcohol after purchasing. Alcohol packaging is becoming more and more attractive to young buyers. Alcopops come in a range of colours and flavours which can be very eye-catching to young people.

Peer pressure: young people may be influenced by their friends encouraging or pressurising them to drink.

Culture: young people are growing up in a 'binge-drinking' culture. Young people's views on alcohol and drunkenness are influenced more and more by culture. If they see others drinking and getting drunk around them, they may be more likely to engage in the activity themselves.

Advertising: advertising alcohol is still legal in the UK. Drink adverts can be seen on TV, billboards, posters and magazines.

Price: promotions such as happy hours or buy one get one free coupled with prices as low as 14p per unit of alcohol have led to government debates about whether alcohol being too cheap encourages young people to drink.

Home environment: approximately 40 per cent of alcoholic drinks sold are drunk at home. The home is a place where young people learn to drink. Parental attitudes to alcohol affect whether or not a young person chooses to drink when they are under eighteen.

Reasons why young people might take up drinking.

| Source A | Information from an online debating website about alcohol |

Alcohol is a harmful drug. It damages our mental and physical health, creates problems for society and is the cause of much violence. These problems are made worse by the availability of cheap alcohol, much of it sold by supermarkets. So is it time to call a halt on cheap booze for the good of us all?

The under eighteen age group has the least amount of disposable income. Raising the price of alcohol to levels which they cannot afford will lower the amount they can afford to buy, if not stop them drinking altogether.

However, as we can see with drug taking, expense and even illegality is no barrier when people want something enough. Making alcohol more expensive will merely make young people who are unable to afford it turn to the black market, or even crime in order to fund it. It is the attitude of the young toward alcohol and their desire for it that needs to be combated, not their ability to 'afford' it.

Debatewise

Activity

1. Using Source A and your own knowledge, evaluate whether cheap alcohol should be banned.

Smoking

In 2007, two-fifths of twelve- to thirteen-year-olds admitted they had tried cigarettes and among fourteen- to fifteen-year-olds the figure was 60 per cent.

(BBC)

Again, the majority of young people know the risks associated with smoking (see page 74) and the warning 'Smoking Kills' could not be missed on cigarette packaging. For young people many of the reasons for taking up smoking are similar to those for drinking alcohol; for example, being affected by parents and peer pressure. Other reasons may include:

- rebellion
- to fit in
- they enjoy it
- experimentation
- to look cool
- to appear more mature
- curiosity
- to control weight
- to deal with stress
- media influence.

The Charity Cancer Research estimates that:

Smoking causes 114,000 deaths in Northern Ireland each year and £5 billion of NHS money is spent on people with smoking-related illnesses in the UK.

The UK government is very keen on reducing this figure and have therefore put measures into place to try to reduce the number of people who smoke. For example:

- In October 2007 the government increased the age for legally buying cigarettes from sixteen to eighteen years of age.
- Most forms of tobacco advertising are banned.
- Cigarettes are heavily taxed.
- In April 2007, the government introduced a law making it illegal to smoke in public places and workplaces.

The government is also considering:

- only allowing cigarettes to be sold from underneath the counter and not having them on display
- banning cigarette vending machines.

Activities

2. Evaluate the impact of the smoking ban and record your discussion by copying and completing the table below.

Advantages of the smoking ban	Disadvantages of the smoking ban

3. Do you think that selling cigarettes from under the counter will have an effect on cigarette sales? Why? Identify and explain **two** reasons for your answer.

Section 2 Concept of self

Learning outcomes

I am learning about:

* identifying personal strengths and weaknesses

* setting targets and working towards goals

* the ability to withstand external pressures that jeopardise health and well-being, future career prospects, family and other close relationships.

As we grow older we go through emotional changes as well as physical changes. We are all influenced by the world around us which helps to shape our personality. Knowing who you are on the inside and finding something you are passionate about is an important part of setting and achieving goals. This section examines how we look at ourselves, the pressures young people are subjected to and how to limit the effect of these pressures, as well as how to set goals and targets in order to achieve the things we want out of life.

Personal strengths and weaknesses

Some people are naturally gifted when it comes to sports, others might shine academically and others might not yet have found where their talents lie. In any case, we all have different strengths, different weaknesses, different talents and a different outlook on the challenges we face. Our outlook on life depends on many factors, including how confident we are in certain tasks, how worthy we feel we are of something but also what kind of mood we are in. This topic looks at each of these individually and what influences them.

What is self-esteem?

Self-esteem is a term used loosely to describe the opinion that you have of yourself. If you have a high opinion of yourself, you have high self-esteem; conversely, a low opinion of yourself equates to low self-esteem. Our opinion of ourselves can change quite rapidly, going from thinking we are wonderful to feelings of despair. Self-esteem is important as it affects how we interact with those around us. Being miserable all

the time is a sign of low self-esteem and might mean people wanting to spend less time with us.

The BBC defines having high self-esteem as:

> ■ *having a positive attitude*
> ■ *valuing ourselves highly*
> ■ *being convinced of our own abilities*
> ■ *seeing ourselves as competent, in control of our own lives and able to do what we want.*

Having a high opinion of yourself is important as it can help you deal with difficult situations and challenges.

What is self-confidence?

Self-confidence is about believing in yourself and believing in your ability to do something. Self-confidence and self-esteem are interrelated; if you have high self-esteem you are more likely to believe in your ability to achieve your goals. Similarly, if you don't feel confident about a particular task, situation or event your negative feelings can become a barrier to success.

What is self-worth?

Self-worth is similar to self-esteem in that it deals with our image of ourselves but is less fickle. Our self-esteem can immediately change from despair to jubilation quite easily whereas self-worth focuses more on our concept of who we are and how we fit into the world in the long-term. Many people judge themselves on how worthy they feel they are of something or whether they feel they have earned something. Self-worth can therefore be thought of in the sense of 'Am I worthy enough to … ?'

Factors that can affect self-confidence, self-esteem and self-worth

Almost everyone is under some kind of pressure or strain at any given time. We can put ourselves under pressure to do well and we can also be influenced by those around us as well as other sources. This is covered in more detail later on pages 86–91 but some of the factors that can influence self-confidence, self-esteem and self-worth are shown in the diagram.

Key words

dyscalculia ■ dyslexia ■ targets

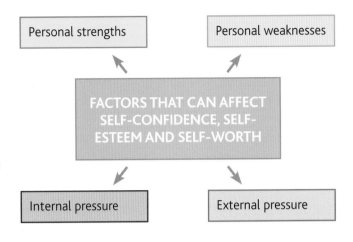

Personal strengths and weaknesses

Everyone has their own individual talents, things that they are good at and things they are not so good at. People tend to enjoy activities and tasks that they are good at, and dislike the things they aren't so good at. For example, if you are good at maths you are more likely to be motivated to do well in class and exams. Being able to identify your own personal strengths and shortcomings can be used to achieve **targets** and goals but also identify things that you can do to improve.

Activities

1. Being realistic about your strengths and weaknesses can improve self-esteem, self-confidence and self-worth. Identify the things you feel are your strengths and weaknesses by copying and completing the table below. An example has been included:

My strengths	My weaknesses	How could I improve my weakness?
Good communicator	Not good at maths	Ask for help, do more practice questions

2. Imagine you are starting a new school. Explain three ways your self-confidence, self-esteem or self-worth could be affected by this experience.

3. Research two learning difficulties – **Dyslexia** and **Dyscalculia** – using the Internet and copy and complete the table below.

	Dyslexia	Dyscalculia
How could this affect a person at school?		
How could this affect a person at work?		
How could this affect a person socially?		
What can be done to help a person overcome this difficulty?		
Name organisations that could help with this difficulty.		
How could this affect a young person's self-esteem, self-confidence and self-worth?		

Targets and goals

Everyone has dreams and aspirations that they would someday like to achieve. Whether your dream is to be a movie star, a pop star, an astronaut, a teacher or a brain surgeon getting there will require effort, dedication and most importantly a plan. Setting goals and targets can help you to reflect on aspirations and plan how best to achieve what you want to do. The words *target* and *goal* are sometimes used interchangeably but it is important to note that, although similar, there is a distinction as explained below.

What is a goal?

A goal is an ambition or something that you would like to achieve in the future. Goals can either be short-term or long-term. For example:

- **Short-term goal:** I want to get 90 per cent or more in my next test.
- **Long-term goal:** I want to be a doctor when I'm older.

What is a target?

In order to achieve your goals it is important to set out a plan. Plans can be made up of individual targets that can be thought of as a series of steps that need to be taken in order to achieve your goals. An example is shown on the right.

What are SMART targets?

When setting targets it is important to keep the end goal in mind. Targets that are **S**pecific, **M**easurable, **A**chievable, **R**ealistic and bound by a **T**ime constraint (**SMART** targets) are more likely to help you to achieve the goal.

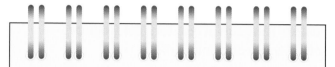

Goal: I want to get five pass grades at GCSE.

Targets:
1. Attend school every day until study leave.
2. Ask questions in class to make sure I understand everything.
3. Do my homework every day.
4. Submit work on time.
5. Make a revision timetable and stick to it.
6. Maintain a healthy work/life balance by playing sport and socialising at least once a week.

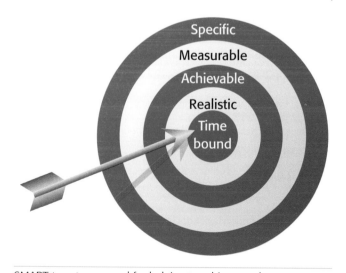

SMART targets are used for helping to achieve goals.

Let's look back at one of the targets to achieve the goal of getting five pass grades at GCSE from the example on page 84. Is it SMART?

Target: 1. *Attend school every day until study leave.*

- Is it **S**pecific? i.e. is it clear and well-defined rather than vague and general, giving you something more definite to aim towards?
  Yes – it is very specific – the aim is to attend school every day.
- Is it **M**easurable? Can you measure whether the target has been achieved or not? Yes – it can be measured by whether the young person goes to school or not.
- Is it **A**chievable? Yes – attending school every day is achievable unless a young person is really ill or has another legitimate reason for not being able to attend school.
- Is it **R**ealistic? Yes – lots of young people have full attendance and usually receive attendance awards or certificates for their efforts. It is not something out of the ordinary that cannot be done.
- Is it **T**ime bound? Yes – the target is to attend school every day until study leave.

Benefits of setting goals

Setting goals can help people achieve what they want in life. The following summarises the benefits of setting goals:

- It helps you to focus on what you want rather than on less important things.
- It helps you to set targets to reach your goals.
- When you know what you want you won't be put off by temporary setbacks.
- You will feel good and have increased self-confidence if you meet the goal.

Rewards

Achieving short-term goals can provide satisfaction and thus be a reward in itself. However, it can be easy to lose sight of long-term goals especially if they are spread out over several years. Setting yourself targets and rewards for reaching those targets can increase your motivation to succeed and help to keep you focused and concentrated on what you want to achieve.

Rewards can vary from small rewards like a night off from studying after a test to big rewards such as a holiday at the end of the school year but they should always be in proportion to the task at hand. Setting big rewards for minimal achievement is not beneficial and will not provide any incentive to achieve long-term goals.

Activities

1. Create a spider diagram of your goals in life – put short-term goals in one colour and long-term goals in another.

2. Take **one** of your goals and set SMART targets for how you can achieve it.

3. Discuss how TV programmes such as *The X-Factor* have given rise to people setting unrealistic goals.

Key word

SMART targets

What pressures do young people face?

There are a lot of pressures exerted on young people in today's society. Pressure is the feeling that someone or something is pushing you towards a particular course of action. Pressure can push us to succeed or it can lead us into taking risks and doing things we wouldn't normally consider. Pressure can come from within ourselves – for example, worrying about exams – or it can come from a variety of external sources. This topic looks at some of the pressures faced by many young people in today's society and some of the factors that contribute towards them.

Common pressures

Common pressures young people face today include:

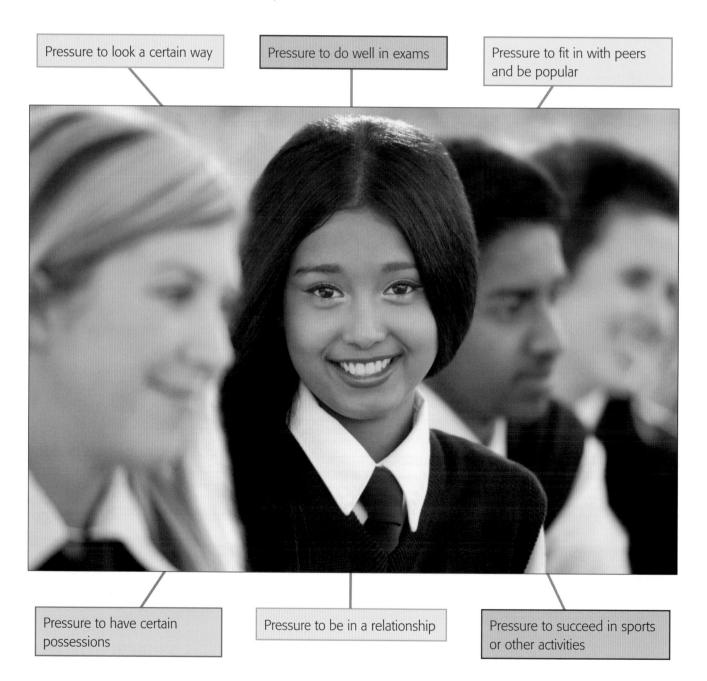

Pressure to look a certain way

Pressure to do well in exams

Pressure to fit in with peers and be popular

Pressure to have certain possessions

Pressure to be in a relationship

Pressure to succeed in sports or other activities

These pressures come from a variety of sources and can affect people in different ways as explained below:

Pressure to look a certain way

One of the biggest pressures that affect young people today is a desire to look a certain way or a desire to be thin – particularly in young women. Sometimes this can lead to spending money on cosmetics or succumbing to the latest fashion trends but it can also lead to **dieting**, stress, cosmetic surgery and eating disorders. The desire to conform to a particular image of beauty can be attributed to numerous factors including the media and peer groups.

Pressure to do well in exams

Exam time can be a very stressful period for young people especially when their exam results can have a significant bearing on their future careers or aspirations. Exam-related stress can be a result of putting yourself under pressure but, additionally, can come from family, peers and also from teacher pressure.

Pressure to fit in with peers

It is human nature to want to be part of a group for various reasons – for example, the need for support from friends, the need for approval, as a way of dealing with insecurity or not wanting to miss out on something. Following the crowd is a normal part of **social development** and can teach us what is or isn't socially acceptable. However, the desire to be accepted by a particular group and to fit in can sometimes lead to your own personal **morals and values** being forgotten and doing things you wouldn't normally do. This kind of pressure usually comes from within but also from peer groups.

Pressure to be popular

We all like to be noticed, to be envied and to be popular and this can be a pressure we put ourselves under, even though more often than not popularity is fickle and fleeting and can lead to anxiety and worry.

Pressure to have certain possessions

Young people can put themselves under pressure to have certain possessions: the latest gadgets, the fastest car, the best mobile phone or the latest high street fashions. Buying such items can be an expensive habit but it can also cause stress and anxiety for young people and their parents. Influence can come from a variety of sources but usually through advertising in the media or from friends and peer groups.

Pressure to be in a relationship

Relationships can be fulfilling and rewarding but they are rarely straightforward and require time and effort to make them work. Young people can find themselves under pressure from various sources to be in relationships, especially sexual relationships.

Young people are quite often curious about sex and this, coupled with hormonal and bodily changes, can result in apprehension about sex or a desire to experience it. Whatever your feelings on the subject, knowing when you are ready is a personal decision and, although pressure can come from within, it can also be influenced by the media, religious beliefs and peers.

Pressure to succeed in sports or other activities

Young people who display a talent for sport, for music, for art or other activities can sometimes find themselves under a lot of pressure to succeed. Sometimes this can stimulate a positive reaction but conversely it can cause stress and discontent. We can put ourselves under excessive pressure to succeed which can be harmful.

Activities

1. Identify and explain **three** ways a young person might try to fit in with peers.

2. Identify and explain **three** ways a young person could overcome peer pressure.

Key words

dieting ■ morals and values ■ social development

How internal and external pressures affect young people

From the previous topic it can be seen that numerous factors can exert pressure on young people, in both a positive and negative way. These include:

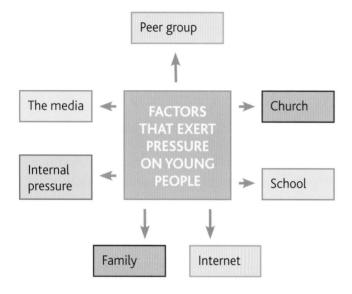

Internal pressure

Many young people put pressure on themselves to be successful or achieve a particular goal. This is referred to as 'internal pressure' and can include exam stress or wanting to look a certain way. Internal pressure can be an invaluable source of inspiration and motivation to achieve goals but it can also lead to stress, low self-esteem, depression or even suicidal thoughts.

Along with *internal* pressures we put ourselves under, there are also *external* pressures that affect young people on a daily basis and these are discussed below.

The media

The media has a big impact on modern society affecting what we see, hear and read. The media includes newspapers, magazines, television, radio, the Internet, mobile phones, billboards, posters and other outlets which seek to inform or entertain. Businesses spend millions of pounds every year on advertising in all possible forms of the media to promote their products and services.

The media can have a positive effect on young people by providing valuable information relating to studies and global affairs as well as helping to increase general knowledge. Further to this, the media can be used to discourage certain behaviours or trends. For example, in early 2010 the sale of the drug mephedrone was banned in the UK thanks in part to a media backlash.

More often than not, however, the media is criticised for how it negatively affects us all, especially young people. It is argued that young people in particular are susceptible to messages conveyed in the media. Television and newspapers regularly depict celebrity lifestyles with a drink- and drug-fuelled culture as something to aspire to. It is also often reported that violence in video games and movies may cause a surge in violence in the streets. However, perhaps the most cause for concern is reserved for how the media portrays beauty. We are all continually subjected to images of models on the front of magazines, in newspapers or on television. Some people fear this has led to an increase in eating disorders in young women.

Peer group

Peer groups and those we choose to associate with can cause pressure and affect how we feel or act. A desire to fit in, to be popular or conform to the values of a particular group has often been cited as a factor in why many young people choose to drink alcohol, smoke and have sex before they are legally allowed to. While peer pressure can contribute to negative actions like this it can also be a positive influence. For example, friends can help talk each other out of risk-taking behaviour such as drug taking.

Religion/Church

Religion and faith can sometimes influence our thinking on many subjects; for example, on contraception or sex before marriage. It can be argued that religion can positively affect young people by instilling in them morals and a sense of right and wrong. Others feel that religions attempt to force opinions, morals and beliefs on their members and that they can subconsciously make people feel guilty about certain activities.

School

School is a considerable part of most young people's lives and directly affects their literacy and numeracy skills and basic knowledge but it can also be a major influence on their social development. Academic success can contribute to higher self-esteem, self-confidence and self-worth whereas stress and pressure exerted by excessive workload, exams, bullying and pressure to succeed both academically and in sporting activities can be detrimental to health and well-being.

The Internet

The Internet has revolutionised the way we communicate and interact socially. Young people in particular spend a lot of time online participating in social networking which can be a good way to keep in touch with friends and meet new people but it can also give rise to **cyber bullying** and other negative effects. The issue of **social networking** is looked at in more detail on pages 92–93.

Family

Family – and parents in particular – can pressurise young people to do well at school, be the best at a sporting activity or to behave at all times. The presence of elder siblings or relatives and constant comparisons to their success can further lead to stress and feelings of inadequacy in a young person. Despite this, however, parents and family can be a source of inspiration and a valuable support network for advice and assistance if or when needed.

Source A	Extract from *Slink – Sex, Love and Life – A to Z of You – Peer Pressure*

Why do people give in to peer pressure?

Most people like to fit in and it's hard being the only one doing something different. Sometimes people are worried they'll be picked on if they don't go with the crowd, or they'll lose their group/gang of friends. Other times people do stuff because they think their friends will like them more, or because their mates are doing it, so it seems normal. You can learn a lot from your peers. They can help you develop your talents and give you support and motivation to succeed. On the other hand, people often end up doing stuff that's bad for them because of the influence of peer pressure, like smoking, missing school or shoplifting.

www.bbc.co.uk/radio1/advice/factfile_az/peer_pressure

Activities

1. Identify and explain **three** ways a young person could cope with pressure.

2. With reference to Source A and your own knowledge, evaluate the impact of peer pressure on a young person's life.

3. Identify and explain **two** reasons why a person may give in to peer pressure.

Key words

cyber bullying ▪ social networking

Strategies for limiting the effects of pressure

The easiest way to minimise the effects of pressure is to limit your exposure to them. This can entail socialising with people you know and trust, watching less TV or talking to parents or teachers if they are pressuring you too much. This topic and the next one look at how certain types of pressure can be reduced.

Exam pressure

In Northern Ireland each year 50,000 pupils sit important exams in year 12 and above. Most of these young people will find themselves experiencing some form of stress during the weeks leading up to exams.

In order to help cope with the pressure of exams, young people should try to take on board some of the following tips:

- Do not leave everything to the last minute.
- Draw up a revision timetable for the months and weeks leading up to the exam.
- Find out what your learning style is, and revise as much as possible using styles that suit you as a learner.
- Make your notes more user-friendly – rewrite the important points, colour them or highlight them.
- Take regular breaks and try to incorporate exercise into these breaks.
- Drink plenty of water and eat a balanced diet to maintain optimum brain function.
- Believe in yourself – you wouldn't be entered for the exam if you were not able to do it.
- Set realistic goals and reward yourself when you have accomplished something.
- Keep things in perspective: exams may seem really important at the time, but in the grander scheme of things, they might not seem as significant. Finally, talk to someone, whether it is a parent or a teacher, so that they can help you deal with pressure.

Bullying

Bullying has been identified as one of the most pressing concerns facing young people in Northern Ireland. In 2005, 75 per cent of young people in Northern Ireland felt that pupils at their school get bullied a little; 10 per cent said pupils get bullied a lot and 30 per cent said they had been bullied themselves.

Bullying damages a young person's self-esteem, self-confidence and self-worth, can leave them depressed, stressed, scared, intimidated and can put them off attending school. There are many ways of dealing with a bully and thus relieving pressure. These include:

- Know it is your right to feel safe and secure in your environment.
- Keep a check on your own anger.
- Practise being confident.
- Stick up for yourself as much as possible.
- Tell someone – for example, your form teacher, year head, pastoral care co-ordinator or a parent or carer.
- Talk to an organisation that can advise you, for example:
  - Bully Busters
  - ChildLine
  - Beatbullying
  - Kidpower

Dieting

Young people are sometimes under pressure to look a certain way and to be thin. Sometimes this can be positive pressure – for example, from a doctor – as going on a diet may be the healthiest option for people who are overweight. However, there are young people who are a healthy weight or underweight but who still put themselves under pressure to be thin for a variety of reasons: peer pressure, the media, or the way they perceive themselves. The stress and anxiety this can cause can lead to dieting, extreme dieting and in some cases eating disorders or **self-harm**.

To alleviate this pressure young people must remind themselves of what is real and what is not real. For example, rich and famous people have time and money to pay personal trainers and dieticians to help them look a certain way and, in addition, many pictures of celebrities are airbrushed to make them look thinner or more attractive before being published.

Young people should stick to a balanced diet and eat the recommended foods in the correct quantities in order to be healthy. They should stay away from any websites or online forums which encourage extreme dieting and eating disorders.

If you are worried about your own eating habits or a friend's, you should always tell a responsible adult in case the condition gets worse. Young people should be proud of what they look like, know people come in all shapes and sizes, and know that happiness comes from within.

Eating disorders

People of all ages can suffer from eating disorders but they are particularly common amongst young people and especially young girls. Many factors contribute to eating disorders including depression, stress, low self-esteem, pressures from family and social pressures from the media. There are two main forms of eating disorder; **anorexia** and **bulimia**. Anorexia nervosa is the term used to describe an obsession with dieting and losing weight. Those suffering from anorexia tend to eat little or no food, take too much exercise or abuse laxatives in order to lose weight. The main difference between anorexia and bulimia is that people who suffer from bulimia tend to eat large amounts of food and then force it out again by being sick or using laxatives. There are many effects of eating disorders which range from fatigue, constipation and dehydration to more serious medical conditions such as heart conditions, low blood pressure, kidney failure and depression.

▲ The media often presents us with examples of the 'perfect' body image.

Key words

anorexia ■ bulimia ■ self-harm

Activities

1. Identify and explain **three** ways young people could deal with: a) parental pressure; and b) peer pressure.

2. Research an anti-bullying organisation and the work that they do and answer the following questions:

   a) Who are they?

   b) What do they do?

   c) Where do they do it?

   d) When are they available?

   e) Why do they do it?

3. Create a revision timetable for any up and coming exams you may have.

4. There are many things in life that young people are very attracted to but which pose great dangers. Dieting is one of them. Copy and complete the table below identifying the attractions and dangers of dieting.

Dieting	
Dangers	**Attractions**

Limiting the effects of social networking on the Internet

More and more young people use the Internet for socialising. This topic looks at what social networking is, how it can benefit young people but also how it can be detrimental to health and well-being.

What is social networking?

'Social networking' is the term used to describe online communication between members of an online community. It includes using instant messaging programs such as AIM, MSN Live or Yahoo! Messenger, chat rooms, forums and sites such as Facebook. Once you sign up for a particular site or service you can begin to socialise with people you know or new people you meet online.

▲ Common UK social networking sites and instant messaging programs.

Social networking has become hugely popular with teenagers and young adults and is now a major method of communication between peers. The table above right shows that of the 36.9 million UK Internet users in May 2009, 29.4 million visited at least one social networking website.

Age profile of UK social networking site category visitors May 2009 Total UK, Age 15+, Home and work locations **Source:** comScore World Metrix		
Age segment	**% reach**	**Average hours per visitor**
Total UK Internet audience	*80%*	*4.6*
Persons: 15–24	86%	5.4
Persons: 25–34	89%	5.4
Persons: 35–44	79%	4.3
Persons: 45–54	77%	3.9
Persons: 55+	67%	3.7

Number of people using social networking in the UK per age group in May 2009

It is clear from this table that social networking is a dominant activity for people of all ages, but particularly in the 15–34 age bracket. Given the popularity and the unsupervised nature of some sites, problems with social networking can occur. Some of the disadvantages are outlined below:

Disadvantages of social networking

1) There have been cases in the past where people have stolen another person's identity online, and pretended to be that person to others. Many people have left themselves signed in only to discover later that someone has used their sign-in to cause damage to their reputation in their absence.
2) People are not always who they say they are online and it has been reported that sexual predators have stalked young people and tried to arrange meetings with them.
3) Social networking sites do not tend to be strict about the comments that are posted. Both good and bad comments can be posted and on many occasions people have become a victim of cyber bullying where a young person has felt intimidated online. This has led to depression and even suicide.
4) A social networking site you might be using is accessible to everyone and can remain online for a long time even after you stop using it. In the future the information it contains can be used by people and prospective employers to make judgements about you.

5) Young people spend a lot of time on social networking sites and the Internet in general. It can become addictive and young people may find themselves in a situation where they don't want to interact face-to-face with other people. Important social skills can become lost and there is now a link between Internet usage and depression.

Advantages of social networking

Despite the dangers there are a lot of advantages to communicating online with friends and peers as listed below:

Search

News

Messages

Events

Friends

Advantages of social networking

1. Building and maintaining friendships.
2. Staying in contact with friends and relatives who live far away.
3. Being reunited with people from the past.
4. Meeting new people.
5. Learning about other people's cultures.
6. Seeing the world from a different point of view.
7. Having your own space on the Internet and being creative with that space.
8. It can be fun.
9. Playing games with others on the same social networking site.
10. Improving IT skills.
11. Improving literacy skills – for example, blogging allows for long passages of writing.

Staying safe online

When online there are steps that you can take to help you stay safe online. These include:

1) Never giving out personal details.
2) Only communicating with real friends.
3) Keeping your social networking site private.
4) Only sharing photos or videos with friends.
5) Never meeting up with anyone you only know from being online.
6) Talking to a parent or carer if someone is talking to you inappropriately.
7) Never accepting files or downloads from people you do not know.
8) Not getting involved in online arguments.

Activity

1. If you were to write home to parents about the dangers their child may face online, what points would you include? What strategies would you tell them to take to limit the dangers? Construct a letter.

Section 3 Building and maintaining healthy relationships

Learning outcomes

I am learning about the positive factors that contribute to the development and maintenance of healthy relationships:

* in families

* amongst a peer group

* in sexual relationships (for example, commitment, mutual respect and willingness to accept responsibility for actions).

A relationship is a connection a person has to another person. Throughout our lifetime we will form, maintain and break relationships with many people including friends, family, partners, classmates, colleagues and members of our local communities. Relationships can be fleeting, lasting only a short time, but some can last a lifetime. This section looks at what factors can contribute to the development and maintenance of common relationships young people face – for example, family relationships, peer relationships and boyfriend/girlfriend relationships.

Relationships

Families

Family relationships can include the relationships we have with our parents, our brothers and sisters but also our extended families such as aunts, uncles, cousins and grandparents. In general, family relationships are built on unconditional love where parents, siblings, etc. love you for who you are and will stand by you through good times and bad. In turn, we love, respect and trust them. Sometimes, however, the relationships we have with family members can be taken for granted and frequently they can become strained especially as we grow up.

▲ The Beckham family

Friendship

Throughout life people establish friendships. The term 'friendship' is used to define the mutual **trust**, co-operation and support between two people. Friendships can range from short-term casual relationships or acquaintances to long-term friendships lasting a lifetime

and tend to be with others with similar interests or jobs, from the same class or the same local community.

Some types of friendship relationships include:

- **Pen pal/e-pal:** someone with whom you correspond via letters/email or social networking sites.
- **Acquaintance:** someone you know but don't spend much time with.

- **Companion:** someone you know and spend time socialising or sharing common activities with but whom you don't consider a close friend.

- **Close friend/best friend:** someone you trust explicitly and share common goals with.

Boyfriend/Girlfriend

The terms 'boyfriend' or 'girlfriend' can be used to define the gender of a friend but generally it refers to the romantic or sexual relationship between two people. Developing and exploring romantic relationships often begins during teenage years when two people form a bond based on attraction. This bond can be used as a basis for developing feelings of love and the intimacy required for a longer lasting commitment such as marriage or a sexual relationship.

Factors affecting relationships

There are several factors that can make a relationship stronger and last longer. These include:

- **Trust:** trust is vital in a relationship. Building up trust can be difficult, particularly if one person has been hurt before. If you trust someone you can tell them everything and depend on them. Without trust one or both of those in a relationship could feel insecure and this could lead to arguments.
- **Mutual respect:** respect in a relationship means that each person values the other person for who they are and understands that the other person has boundaries which should not be challenged.
- **Honesty:** being open and honest is an essential part of building trust within a relationship. If one person withholds information from the other for any reason then they are not being totally honest and, in turn, have doubts about the relationship. Not being honest can lead to feelings of guilt and can have repercussions if it comes to light.

- **Communication:** it is almost impossible to have a relationship without communication. Communication – verbal or nonverbal – is important for expressing opinions, values, beliefs, ideas, feelings and thoughts and is a two-way process.
- **Degree of independence:** people involved in a relationship need to give each other space and time to themselves. People need to grow and develop individually but it can be very easy to fall into a routine of spending all one's spare time with the other person which can lead to boredom and arguments.
- **Compromise:** you need to have give-and-take in a relationship. It is important that all decisions in a relationship are made together and that one person does not get their own way all the time. To compromise is to 'meet in the middle' and come to a conclusion that both people in the relationship are happy with.
- **Tolerance:** everyone has bad habits and no one is perfect. Being tolerant of someone means putting up with things that annoy you.
- **Willingness to accept responsibility:** it is the responsibility of both people in a relationship to ensure that everything that happens will not be regretted in the future. It is important to not play the 'blame game' and hold other people responsible if something goes wrong.
- **Commitment:** being committed is when two people make a pledge to stay together through good times and bad times and do not give up easily. If the two people involved are committed then the relationship will be more stable and more likely to last.

Activities

1. Look at the factors affecting relationships above and try to identify **three** more important factors that you think every relationship should have. Explain your answer.

2. 'It is important that a child has two parents who have a good relationship.' Do you agree or disagree with this statement? Identify and explain **three** reasons for your answer.

Key words

acquaintance ■ pen pal ■ e-pal ■ trust

Section 4 Recognising, assessing and managing risk

Learning outcomes

I am learning about the risks and benefits for a young person recognising and assessing risks with regards to:

* parents
* peer group
* school
* the media.

Risk taking behaviour is when a person takes on a challenge that may or may not have a desirable outcome. It is possible to take calculated risks – for example, an entrepreneur taking on a new business venture – however, more often than not, risk taking is used to describe uncalculated and unhealthy behaviour. Some risk taking can have long-term consequences on health – for example, taking drugs – and some can even put others' lives in danger.

What sort of risks do young people take?

The diagram below shows some examples of risks some young people take:

Activity

1. Copy and complete the table by putting together the benefits and costs of risks taken by young people.

Activity	Benefits	Costs
Joyriding		
Taking drugs		
Unprotected sex		
Drinking and driving		
Shoplifting		
Deliberate self-harm		
Sunbathing		
Lifts with strangers		
Fighting		

Why do young people take risks?

Peer pressure: the main source of inspiration for young adults to take risks is peer pressure and a desire to impress those within the same peer group. Young people aspire to be unique but also have a strong need to be accepted. This need can result in adopting the values and beliefs of a peer group and taking part in activities that would normally be considered immoral or risky.

Rebelling against parents: it can be argued that acting out against parents is a natural part of growing up. Our parents are possibly the biggest influence on our early development and control most of what we do. If this controlling is seen as negative and restrictive it can lead to young people acting out or taking a risk to prove a point or gain attention.

Curiosity: young people like to experience new things and this could lead to them indulging their curiosities about alcohol and drugs.

Being under the influence of alcohol or drugs: being under the influence of substances such as alcohol and drugs can alter brain activity and cloud judgement. Not being able to think clearly and rationally can make people more open to suggestion and less likely to consider the consequences of their actions.

Boredom: boredom may tempt a young person into doing something they deem to be exciting. They may partake in activities that seem fun initially, but could be risky. For example, pier jumping.

School: school is designed and structured to be a place of learning and development for all but sometimes can be seen as restricting, tedious, repetitive and boring to some pupils. It is often difficult to express individuality at school so pupils may act out and rebel which can lead to suspension or expulsion.

The media: as discussed on page 88, what we read in newspapers, hear on the radio or see on TV can lead to us taking risks especially if it is perceived that it is low risk and will be fun. For example, we often hear of celebrities with drug problems in the media which may influence young people into trying drugs also.

How to avoid risk-taking behaviour

Risk taking behaviour has been identified as a normal part of growing up, where young people learn from their mistakes and develop into more mature people. It is important that young people minimise any potential harm to themselves and others while undergoing this period in their life. This can be done by talking to parents, evaluating risk taking behaviour, choosing friends carefully or taking on safer activities.

Parental/carer support

If you are considering involving yourself in something risky, you should talk to parents or carers. Parents/carers have your best interests at heart. They were also young once and could offer advice on how to deal with tricky situations or practical ways of avoiding the situation altogether.

Self-evaluation of risk

Understand and balance the advantages of risk taking behaviour against the disadvantages and weigh up the likelihood of getting a desirable outcome. If the risk taking behaviour is thought through and deemed unsafe, then it should be avoided.

Choose friends carefully

Pick your friends based on common interests and personality compatibility and avoid the people who do not accept you for who you are or those who you continually have to impress.

Channel energies into safer activities

It's good to have a hobby or a pastime you enjoy. This way there is less chance of getting bored and wanting to do something risky. If you crave an adrenalin rush engage in an activity – for example, a sport – that gives you it without risking yourself or others.

Section 5 Understanding the roles and responsibilities of parenting

Learning outcomes

I am learning about the challenges faced by young parents, for example:

* emotional issues
* financial issues
* career prospects.

Becoming a parent is a life-changing experience. It can be greatly rewarding and satisfying to bring a new life into the world and watch a child grow up, but it can also be daunting and stressful especially for young people and new parents. This section looks at the legal responsibilities parents have when it comes to raising children and at some of the issues that young parents might face.

Parenting

Becoming a parent is not an easy time. Young parents in particular may find the changes a baby brings very challenging. Young people may be unaware of what is expected of them as a parent especially if the child had been unplanned. The United Nations Convention on the Rights of a Child (UNCRC) outlines the rights each child should have (see page 31).

A parent should ensure that their child's rights are being met and they have a responsibility to make sure this happens. The main roles and responsibilities of a parent are shown on page 99.

Activities

1. Look at the information on page 99. Are there any other things a parent or carer does for you that you think should be included in the main roles and responsibilities of a parent? Give your reasons.

2. Draw up a charter of rights and responsibilities for parents.

3. Identify and explain **three** advantages of having children while you are still young.

1. A parent is expected to provide a **safe environment**. For example:
   - keep the child safe from abuse
   - keep unsafe objects away from the child
   - safety proof the home.

2. A parent is expected to provide a **loving environment**. For example:
   - spend time with the child
   - communicate with the child
   - show an interest in the child
   - be affectionate towards the child.

3. A parent is expected to **financially support** the child. Until the child turns eighteen a parent is expected to spend money on the needs of the child. For example, lunch money, money for school trips and money for the basic needs of the child.

9. A parent is expected to **discipline a child**. For example:
   - reward good behaviour
   - be consistent with punishing bad behaviour
   - be fair.

8. A parent is expected to **encourage and foster interests and skills**. For example,
   - encourage a child to participate in a club
   - acknowledge achievement in their interest
   - set realistic expectations
   - make an interest or a skill into something fun, not something that they dislike doing.

4. A parent is expected to help support a child's **educational needs**. For example:
   - communicate regularly with the school
   - help with homework
   - celebrate the child's achievement at school
   - have conversations with the child about what goes on at school.

5. A parent is expected to provide for the child's **basic needs**. For example, ensure the child has:
   - water
   - food
   - clothes
   - shelter
   - a warm bed
   - medical care.

7. A parent is expected to provide **opportunities for social development**. For example:
   - organise play dates
   - encourage making friends
   - encourage the child to talk about their feelings
   - bring the child to places where there will be other children – for example, the park.

6. A parent is expected to assist with the **development of a child's morals and values**. For example:
   - teach the child the difference between right and wrong
   - lead by example and show the importance of values such as honesty, respect, patience, generosity and forgiveness.

Young parents

While some teenagers intend to get pregnant, research shows that the majority of teenage pregnancies are accidental and unplanned. In Northern Ireland the numbers of teenage pregnancies have decreased since 2001. The table below shows the number of births to mothers under the age of twenty from 2001 to 2007.

Year	Number
2000	1,614
2001	1,524
2002	1,502
2003	1,484
2004	1,486
2005	1,395
2006	1,427
2007	1,405
2008	1,426

Source: www.nisra.gov.uk

Raising children is one of life's most rewarding roles but it can also pose numerous challenges. Parents in their teens often face the most difficult challenges as they are still maturing themselves. Over time many young parents may face emotional, social and financial issues.

Emotional issues

Having a baby can be an emotionally trying time for any parent but can be especially difficult for young parents. Studies show that they are more likely to face issues such as postnatal depression, stress and fear of failure. Other emotional problems that can arise are social stigma and the loss of social interaction.

Social stigma

Being a teenage parent is more socially acceptable now than it would have been in the past. However, some young parents still feel that they are frowned upon by society. Some people feel that a young parent is unable to care for a child when they are still a child themselves. Young parents are often seen as a drain on the welfare system and many working adults feel resentful that the tax they pay is being spent on what they perceive to be reckless teenagers. There are also people who think young parents lack sense in getting themselves into the situation, while some older members of society may feel that having a child without being married is shameful. **Social stigma** can lower self-confidence and self-esteem and cause a young parent to be embarrassed about their situation.

Social life

Once a baby is born it takes up copious amounts of time and energy. A young person will not be able to interact with friends or take part in the same social activities as other young people their age. Finding someone to look after the child may also prove difficult and therefore time spent socialising can be dramatically reduced which can affect emotional and social health.

Financial issues

Raising a child can be very expensive. Costs such as clothing, food, nappies, childcare, prams, cots, toys, medical care and everything else that children require very quickly mounts up. Young parents may have to rely on family, friends and benefits to help with costs and also childcare which can add to stress and be emotionally challenging.

Career prospects

The job market is a highly competitive place. Young people in particular may find it difficult to find a job without work experience and qualifications. As explained on the following page, staying in full-time education can be difficult for young parents and they may need to forsake long-term career plans to take any available employment. However, there are numerous options that parents can benefit from to help them care for their children. These include: **maternity leave, paternity leave**, career breaks, part-time hours and flexible working hours. For more information on careers and job prospects in particular refer to pages 112–69.

School

A young parent's education will be dramatically affected by having a child. During pregnancy the young woman may find it difficult to attend school as often as they would have done and may fall behind. If this happens before important exams they may not fully achieve their goals and reach their academic potential.

After becoming a parent, a young woman may be unable to attend school at all as the child will become their main priority. Those who try to balance parenthood with school will be at a disadvantage as time spent at home will be centred on the child and homework may become neglected. Most infants do not settle into regular sleeping patterns until they are older and this could mean that the young parent will be sleeping less at night. This will affect how often the young parent can come to school and will also affect concentration while at school.

Health

Teenage mothers can face both emotional and physical health problems. The death rate from pregnancies in young people under fifteen is much higher due to a higher risk of complications. Teenage mothers are more likely to suffer premature or prolonged labour and if the bone structure is not fully developed, they take the risk of injuring their spine and pelvic bones. Being a mother and taking care of a baby is a demanding job, and can be emotionally draining. If young mothers are unprepared for the arrival of the child, the vast change in lifestyle could result in depression.

Absence of a father

Teenage relationships generally do not last because as you get older you meet new people, learn new things about yourself, and your personality and preferences change. Therefore, some teenage mothers can find themselves alone while bringing up a child, without the help of the father. This can be particularly stressful as all the responsibility of parenting lies with one person and this can be a very lonely time for a young mother.

Activities

4. Brook and Barnardo's are two organisations which can help young mothers. Find out how they can help teenage parents. The following websites may help you:
   - www.brook.org.uk
   - www.barnardos.org.uk

5. In pairs, decide on a list of essential items every newborn requires. Use a catalogue/the Internet to help you. Find out the cost of the items and add it up. Does the total surprise you? Why?

6. 'If you fall pregnant you should get married.' Using your own knowledge, assess whether a teenage couple should adhere to this statement.

▲ Teenage parents often face many difficult challenges.

Key words

maternity leave ■ paternity leave ■ social stigma

Section 6 Developing competence as discerning consumers

Learning outcomes

I am learning about common financial terms, the advantages and disadvantages of consumer choices and managing a budget, for example issues of:

＊ quality versus price

＊ cash versus credit

＊ buy versus rent

＊ new versus second-hand.

We all use money on a daily basis. People go to work to earn money and then in turn they spend it on things they want or need or save it for a rainy day. This section looks at the common terms that are often used by banks and businesses relating to money, what choices we have as consumers, how a budget can help a person manage their money and how debt problems can be addressed.

Key terms relating to money

Like it or not, money is an essential part of daily life. We make money and in turn spend money on things such as food, clothing, entertainment, travel and housing. Below are some common terms regularly used when talking about money.

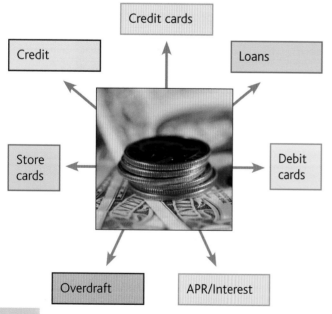

- Credit cards
- Credit
- Loans
- Store cards
- Debit cards
- Overdraft
- APR/Interest

Credit

Credit is a term used to describe obtaining goods or services without paying for them immediately or paying in instalments. Different types of credit include loans, credit cards and store cards.

Credit card

Credit cards are a commonly accepted form of payment for goods and can also be used to withdraw cash. Organisations such as MasterCard and Visa agree to give people credit up to a certain limit and, in turn, send out monthly bills with a minimum amount to be repaid. If credit card bills are paid off in full each month then there is little or no charge for the consumer. However, if people fail to pay off the full balance then they are charged interest on the money they owe which adds to their debt. Credit cards can be useful when purchasing items online as they offer the consumer more protection if the item doesn't arrive. For example, if something you bought was not delivered the credit card company would issue a refund.

▲ Common credit card companies.

Store card

Most major retailers offer a form of credit card called a store card, which you can only use with that particular shop or retail group. Store cards can be useful, and often come with tempting offers, but they can also be very expensive as they often have high interest levels.

Debit card

When debit cards are used they take out (debit) the value of the goods or services from the bank account linked to the card. When using a debit card it is often easy to spend more money than is in the account. This would mean that you go into an overdraft.

Loan

A **loan** is an agreement between a borrower and a lender to provide a sum of money upfront that is to be repaid later. Typically loans are repaid in instalments and as such the borrower is charged interest payments. Commonly loans are provided by banks, building societies and credit unions to help people buy expensive items such as a new car or a house.

Loans can be secured against the item being bought (e.g. against a new car) or they can be unsecured (e.g. a bank overdraft). If managed correctly with manageable repayments, loans can be an invaluable source of money.

Overdraft

An overdraft is a type of unsecured loan provided by a bank or building society. An overdraft is a set amount of money that can be borrowed by the account holder if required. Unfortunately, there are usually charges for using such a service and any money borrowed can be subject to interest charges too.

Loan shark

Loan sharks tend to offer loans with high interest rates and to operate outside the law – using the threat of violence or blackmail on people they have lent money to. Loan sharks can seem like a good option when other sources of income are unavailable but they are high risk and should be avoided if possible.

APR/interest

Charging interest on money owed is how credit card companies and other lenders make a **profit** from lending people money. If you take out a loan and repay it over a period of time you will generally have paid more than the original sum you borrowed. The higher the interest rate and longer the term of repayment the more the borrower will have to repay.

APR stands for Annual Percentage Rate and represents the interest charges over one year. By law anyone lending money has to declare the APR which makes it easier for borrowers to compare loans and see how much they will be charged. Like interest rates, the lower the APR the better for the borrower.

Debt

Generally speaking the term 'debt' is used to describe an amount of money that a person owes to other people or organisations. Debt can be accumulated from **mortgages**, personal loans, credit card debt, store cards and many other sources.

Budget

Budgets can be used by individuals, households, businesses and governments and are an invaluable tool used to manage money coming in (income) and money spent (**expenditure**).

Activities

1. Research the following terms using the Internet and determine the main differences between them:

   a) current account • savings account

   b) bank • building society

2. Is a mortgage a secured or unsecured loan? Explain your answer.

Key words

budget ▪ credit ▪ expenditure ▪ loan ▪ mortgage ▪ profit

Budgeting

Budgets are an invaluable tool for managing finances. They are used by governments and businesses to manage income (money coming in) and expenditure (spending) on a weekly/monthly/yearly basis. A budget is a money plan and can be used on a smaller scale by individuals to manage their own finances. This section looks at what information a budget contains, how to stick to a budget and the advantages of using one.

Making and using a personal budget

There is no right or wrong way to make a budget but most contain a list of all available income and all expenditures whether necessary or optional. Necessary spending includes things that we need – for example, rent or food.

When essential things have been paid for, the money left over can be used for things you want, like new clothes or spending the money on going on holiday. As we get older sources of income and expenditures change (e.g. mortgage repayments or car repairs).

An example of a budget a young person may have is shown below:

	Week 1 (£)	Week 2 (£)	Week 3 (£)	Week 4 (£)	Monthly total (£)
Income					
Wages from part-time job	20	20	0	20	60
Pocket money	5	5	5	5	20
Selling items online	10	0	0	25	35
Benefits	0	0	0	0	0
Other	80	0	0	10	90
Total income	**115**	**25**	**5**	**60**	**205**
Spending					
Mobile phone bill	10	10	10	10	40
Savings	20	0	0	0	20
Food	10	10	10	10	40
Clothing	60	0	0	0	60
Entertainment	5	10	5	5	25
Other	0	0	0	0	0
Total expenditure	**105**	**30**	**25**	**25**	**185**
Net Income	10	-5	-20	35	20

Net income is calculated by subtracting total expenditure from total income. In order to save money on a regular basis or help get out of debt, total expenditure should be greater than total income. If net income is negative then you need to increase income somehow or spend less. In the example shown above, net income at the end of the month is £20.

Budgets are flexible. Many are updated on a monthly basis but it can sometimes be easier to break them down into weeks or even days to obtain a better understanding of how much you spend. The more often a budget is updated the more likely it is to be accurate and the more beneficial it will be.

Advantages of budgeting

Some of the advantages of making and keeping a budget include:

- makes it easier to track and control spending
- shows where you are spending too much
- can relieve money-related stress
- can help with debt management
- can help free up and save money
- can help with investing money
- can help prepare for emergencies
- can help share financial information with others – for example, couples can track spending or have it to hand if such information is required when applying for a loan or mortgage.

Keeping to a budget

Keeping to a budget can be difficult; however, the diagram below gives some tips on keeping on track.

Finally, do it now rather than later. Creating a budget sooner rather than later can set you on the way to achieving your goals.

Activities

3. Create a table detailing your own income and spending for:

   a) today   **b)** this week   **c)** this month.

   What is your net income at the end of each of these?

4. 'A budget is a beneficial tool that makes life easier.' Evaluate the impact of a budget on a young person's life.

5. Refer to the sample budget on page 104:

   a) What could the person do to increase income?

   b) What could the person do to decrease spending?

   c) If the person lost their part-time job but carried on spending the same how would this affect their net income?

6. What other expenditures would adults have compared to young people?

Motivation: when creating a budget and trying to stick to it, it is important to keep in mind the motivation you have for changing your spending habits and the goals you want to achieve.

Keep your budget up to date: keeping track of spending on a daily basis can help keep your budget up to date. Regularly checking and updating the budget will help keep you focused on your goals but will also allow you to make any necessary changes.

Treat yourself: it is important to socialise and put aside money for the fun things in life. If you are making a budget it is important to factor in time and money for entertainment which can help keep you motivated. Additionally, it is important to set yourself regular rewards especially if your budget is spread out over a long period of time.

STICKING TO A BUDGET

Be realistic: when creating a budget it is important to be realistic about what you can afford to save or pay off. Trying to save too much can mean taking money away from other expenditures.

Consider quality vs price: cheaper items can sometimes be inferior quality and better quality items tend to cost more. It is important to research items to see if you can save money elsewhere and what represents the best value for money. This is covered in more detail on page 106.

Self-discipline: perhaps the hardest thing to do is to be self-disciplined. Changing your spending habits takes a lot of will power but over time it is possible to adjust to the lifestyle your budget calls for.

Key words

net income

Consumer choices

We all need to buy different products and pay for services throughout our lifetime. Whether we are buying relatively cheap items in a local shop or buying a house there is almost always a range of choices available. These choices can be summarised into the following categories:

- quality versus price
- cash versus credit
- new versus second-hand
- needs versus wants
- buy versus rent.

Quality versus price

Everyone wants to get the best possible value for their money. It is often thought that the more something costs the better quality it will be and the longer it will last. However, this is not always the case and therefore it is important to know how much you can afford then shop around to get the best possible quality without overspending.

Cash versus credit

Most retailers or service providers have facilities to pay by cash or by credit or debit card. But what are the advantages or disadvantages of each type of payment? The table below lists the advantages and disadvantages of cash and credit.

One of the main advantages of using a credit card is the fact that it offers a lot more protection to buyers when shopping online. If you buy something online with a credit card and it doesn't arrive, your credit card company will refund the amount paid and then charge the retailer.

New versus second-hand

Buying something brand new, unwrapping it, testing it, setting it up and showing it off can give a great sense of satisfaction and pride. When purchasing goods such as white goods (e.g. fridges, washing machines, etc.) people will often buy new and won't consider buying second-hand. Generally a new item will last longer, represents better value for money and often comes

Advantages	Disadvantages
Cash	
Can make budgeting/accounting easier	Less convenient, might have to search for an ATM
Handing over cash tends to lead to less spending	If you lose your wallet/purse, any cash in it might never be returned
Less likely to be subject to identity fraud	Carrying a large amount of cash can make you a target for criminals
Debit cards	
More convenient than cash	Can lead to overspending if not managed carefully
Can track spending with online banking	Can be subject to criminals stealing account information or ID fraud
Can be used to shop online	Some retailers/ATMs charge for using a debit card
Can be replaced if lost/stolen	Doesn't have same payment protection as a credit card
Credit cards	
More convenient than cash	Can lead to overspending if not managed carefully
Credit can be easily obtained	Can lead to debt
Can track spending online	Some companies charge a monthly fee
Buyer protection means you are less likely to be subject to online scams	Can be expensive if interest rates are high
Can be replaced if lost/stolen	Credit cards can be an easy target for criminals
Good credit history can make it easier to obtain a loan/mortgage	Onus is on customer to resolve any credit history disputes

The advantages and disadvantages of cash, debit cards and credit cards.

with a warranty or guarantee should anything go wrong. However, this peace of mind comes with a higher price tag which can put it outside the purchasing power of many people. In this case buying used goods is the only option. This is especially true with large purchases such as cars. Most people are aware that buying a new car is expensive and that the resale value decreases quite radically as soon as you take ownership. Buying a second-hand car is cheaper but it can be quite stressful trying to find a good quality car at a reasonable price. However, finding a good bargain can be just as satisfying as buying new.

Needs versus wants

There is a wide variety of products and services available on the market all competing for our money. With all the choices available it can be quite easy to buy the things we want and not have enough left over to buy the things we actually need. Therefore it is important to understand the difference. A **need** is something that is essential for surviving and includes such things as food, water, clothing and shelter. In Northern Ireland, the standard of living is quite high and so services such as electricity, heating and medical facilities can also be considered a necessity. In comparison, **wants** are luxuries that we can do without but would like in order to enhance our lifestyles and make life more enjoyable. Luxuries include things such as MP3 players, mobile phones, holidays, computers, alcohol and cars. Spending money on what we actually need should always be a priority before spending on the things we want.

Key words

needs ▪ wants

Activities

1. Think of something you or someone else has bought second-hand. Was it a good experience or a bad experience? Explain your answer.

2. On the right is a shopping list for a pupil going back to school after the summer. Decide if the items listed are needs or wants.

3. Look at the same list and imagine the pupil was returning to school after the Christmas holidays. Has anything changed? If so, why?

4. 'Using a credit card is useful when short of money.' Evaluate the impact of a person using a credit card.

Item	Need	Want
New uniform		
Laptop computer		
New school shoes		
New trainers		
New coat		
New schoolbag		
New lunchbox		
New pencil case + stationery		
File paper		
Latest mobile phone		
New cosmetics/beauty products		

Buy versus rent

Generally it is possible to rent most goods such as a TV, fridge or a car if you don't have the money to buy them outright. Paying a few pounds a week to rent a TV means you don't have to worry about it breaking down as the rental company will replace it but it will also mean you will never own the item and will lose out on any potential profits should you ever need to sell it.

The decision to buy or rent is an important one when it comes to accommodation or housing. Many people aspire to own their own home but for many it makes more economic sense to live in rented accommodation.

Numerous factors affect decision-making when it comes to buying or renting accommodation and some of these are shown in the diagram on the right.

Buying a house or property can be very stressful and can take several months to complete. It involves numerous parties other than the sellers and buyers, such as estate agents, surveyors and solicitors. Buying is a long-term commitment but has many advantages and disadvantages as shown in the diagram below:

Costs: can you afford to repay a mortgage, pay insurance and maintain and repair a house by yourself?

Time scales: how long do you want to live in a certain area before moving on?

Area: it may not be affordable to buy in some desirable areas whereas renting might be worth considering.

BUY/RENT

Current interest rates for mortgages: interest rates might be very high or very low and this will affect the mortgage repayments and whether or not you can afford them.

State of the housing market: the average price of buying a house varies and may go up or down. Deciding to rent because you believe house prices will drop is a gamble but might be worthwhile.

Factors affecting choices when deciding to buy a house or rent.

Advantages

- Greater sense of independence and increased self-esteem.
- You own the property so can make improvements or build extensions.
- It is possible to rent out rooms or your driveway to generate extra income.
- You can turn your house into a business – for example, a B&B.
- Any improvements made are likely to increase the value of the property.
- Selling the house for more than the purchase price can lead to big profits.
- Home owners tend to have a higher social standing.

Disadvantages

- Many people don't have the capital (money) to buy a house and so need to take out a mortgage.
- Mortgage repayment rates can vary and generally have high interest rates so you end up paying a lot more than you borrowed.
- Failing to keep up with mortgage repayments can mean losing your house.
- The value of the house can decrease meaning you would lose money if it was resold. In this case you may be repaying a mortgage for more than the value of the property (this is referred to as '**negative equity**').

Advantages and disadvantages of buying a house.

If you choose to rent accommodation you become a **tenant** and the person you rent from becomes your landlord. You will be required to sign a **rental agreement** which states the conditions of rental, for example, how much rent will be paid and what the landlord is responsible for. University students who live away from home tend to rent accommodation as it is cheaper and the house may come fully furnished. Other advantages and disadvantages of renting include:

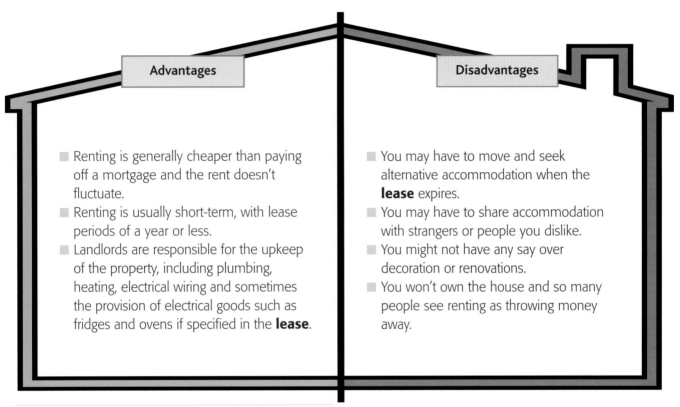

Advantages

- ▥ Renting is generally cheaper than paying off a mortgage and the rent doesn't fluctuate.
- ▥ Renting is usually short-term, with lease periods of a year or less.
- ▥ Landlords are responsible for the upkeep of the property, including plumbing, heating, electrical wiring and sometimes the provision of electrical goods such as fridges and ovens if specified in the **lease**.

Disadvantages

- ▥ You may have to move and seek alternative accommodation when the **lease** expires.
- ▥ You may have to share accommodation with strangers or people you dislike.
- ▥ You might not have any say over decoration or renovations.
- ▥ You won't own the house and so many people see renting as throwing money away.

Advantages and disadvantages of renting accommodation.

As can be seen, deciding whether to buy or rent is a personal decision and depends on your personal and financial circumstances at the time. Many people desire to be on the **property ladder** but this can come at a cost.

Key words

lease ▪ negative equity ▪ property ladder ▪ rental agreement ▪ tenant

Activities

5. You have decided to rent a house – what do you think would be your main expenditures?

6. What do you think would be the main expenditures if you bought a house?

7. You are about to attend university and decide to buy a house. Evaluate the decision to do so.

Debt

The term 'debt' is generally used to describe when you owe someone money. However, all debt is not necessarily bad – for example, many people to go into debt when taking out a mortgage to buy a house. Debt can become a problem when a person owes a lot of money, possibly to several lenders, and when they struggle to repay them.

How people fall into debt

People can fall into debt for many reasons, as shown below:

Poor health: if you are not able to work you won't be able to earn money and may have medical/care bills to pay.

Poor budgeting: spending more than you earn may mean going into debt in order to pay bills.

Loss of a job: losing a job will affect household income meaning difficulty in paying bills or meeting repayments.

HOW PEOPLE FALL INTO DEBT

Unexpected spending: unforeseen expenditures – for example, a car repair – may take a person by surprise and they may need to borrow money to pay the bill.

Increase in the size of a family: an unexpected pregnancy or an elderly/sick relative coming to live with a family will increase the amount of money that has to be spent within the household. This could mean a family may have to borrow money to cope with the added pressure.

Gambling addiction: a person who is addicted to gambling may be unable to stop despite the negative consequences and can run up large debts.

Drug addiction: drug addicts will beg, borrow or steal to feed their drug habit which can lead to debt.

Consequences of debt

When debt spirals out of control it can have serious repercussions including:

Legal consequences

When you borrow money, you enter into a legal agreement whereby you have an obligation to repay the amount you borrowed at a set rate of interest over a specific period of time. The courts can declare you bankrupt if you fail to meet repayments.

Loss of property

If you use your house as security against a loan or mortgage it may be at risk if you fail to keep up with repayments. Similarly, if you do not meet your rent payments the landlord can seek legal help to **evict** you.

Social stigma of debt

People with debt issues are sometimes looked down upon and are thought to be unable to manage money. Those who are in debt greatly fear a negative reaction from their family and friends to their situation which can add to stress.

Emotional health

The stress and worry caused by debt can leave a person emotionally unwell. It can lead to depression and anxiety and, in some cases, suicide.

Crime

If a person feels that they cannot pay off their debts legally, they make look at illegal options. They could, for example, turn to theft or drug dealing in order to pay off their loans.

Spiral into further debt

Many people in debt can struggle to pay for essential everyday items and in turn borrow money from friends, family or loan sharks. Borrowing money to pay off debt is risky and is often referred to as the 'debt cycle' as shown in the diagram below:

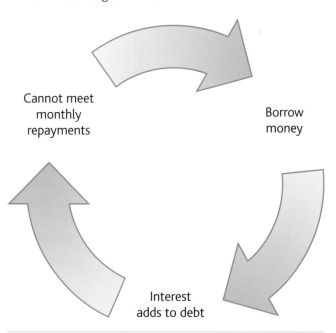

The debt cycle.

Coping with debt and becoming debt-free

Getting out of debt isn't easy and can take a long time depending on how much money is owed and the interest charges and fees that are incurred. There are many methods that can help alleviate the burden of debt including:

- **Seeking advice:** organisations such as the **Consumer Credit Counselling Service (CCCS) or Citizens Advice Bureau (CAB)** can provide free impartial advice on how best to cope with debt.
- **Talking to family and friends:** talking through problematic debts and possible strategies can help reduce stress.
- **Evaluating your budget:** re-examine or create a personal budget to further reduce expenditure/increase income.
- **Talking to the creditor:** this can lead to a revised payment plan or payment schedule.
- **Consolidating loans:** some companies offer debt consolidation whereby they will take control of all your debts and you pay them a set amount each month. This means only dealing with one company and can be beneficial depending on how much they charge.
- **Shopping around:** try to move loans or only borrow from organisations with the lowest interest rates.
- **Bankruptcy:** this is a drastic step, but if all else fails a person can declare themselves bankrupt. This means they will no longer have to pay their debts but it has a certain social stigma attached to it and it may be difficult to borrow money in the future.

Activities

1. People sometimes turn to loan sharks to get themselves out of debt. Evaluate their decision to do so.

2. Explain why you think people might find it difficult to ask for help when in debt.

3. Pretend that you are a debt counsellor for either the Consumer Credit Counselling Service (www.cccs.co.uk) or Citizens Advice Bureau (www.citizensadvice.org.uk). Research their website so you can explain how your organisation can help people in debt.

Key words

bankruptcy ▪ Citizens Advice Bureau (CAB) ▪ Consumer Credit Counselling Service (CCCS) ▪ creditor ▪ eviction

Section 1 The impact of globalisation on employment

Learning outcomes

I am learning about the impact of global economic changes on Northern Ireland, for example:

* changing employment patterns
* migration and immigration
* the growth of new technologies.

This section looks at the impact of global economic changes on Northern Ireland. It explores how global economic changes have led to changes in employment patterns and examines their impact on migration and immigration. Finally, it investigates how the growth of new technologies has had an impact on Northern Ireland.

Globalisation

Globalisation is the movement of goods, people and ideas around the world. Products such as cars, furniture, chocolate bars, etc. are referred to as goods.

Many companies produce and sell their goods throughout the world. For example, Cadbury is owned by Kraft, an American company – it produces Dairy Milk in England, using cocoa beans from Ghana, and sells it in over 30 countries throughout the world.

As well as products moving throughout the world, many people migrate to live in different countries in search of employment. For example, in 2009, 567,000 people came as immigrants to the UK, whereas 368,000 people emigrated from the UK. Movement of people and developments in technology such as the Internet mean that new ideas also flow throughout the world much more quickly than before.

▲ A bar of chocolate that you buy in your local shop has ingredients from many different countries and is sold all over the world. It is a global product.

Activities

1. Before a chocolate bar arrives in the shops the ingredients have been harvested and processed in a number of different places. Find out how a bar of Cadbury's milk chocolate is made and where it is sold, and then complete the factfile about the bar:

JOURNEY OF A CHOCOLATE BAR	
a) Where do the cocoa beans come from?	
b) Where does the milk come from?	
c) Where do the cocoa beans go to when they've been harvested?	
d) Where is the chocolate bar made?	
e) Where is the chocolate bar sold?	

2. Explain how your factfile about chocolate shows an example of globalisation.

Imports and exports

As we have seen, chocolate made in England is exported to many countries throughout the world. Export means that goods and or services from one country are sold to other countries.

The companies in other countries that buy products from the UK are said to be 'importing' the products. Import means that goods and or services are brought into the country from another country. They can be complete goods such as bananas, pineapples, etc. or partly finished goods such as iron for aeroplane parts.

In the UK we import and export goods and services to many different countries, and this exchange of goods provides employment.

The biggest exporters to the UK in 2009 were Germany, USA, China, Netherlands and France (the total value of UK imports in 2009 was £306bn). The biggest importers from the UK in 2009 were the USA, Germany, Netherlands, France and Ireland (the total value of UK exports in 2009 was £224bn).

Top five UK exports	Top five UK imports
Medicines	Cars
Petrol	Petrol
Cars	Aerospace
Other oils	Telecoms
Engines/motors	Medicines

The top UK exports and imports in 2009

▲ Some of the top British exports include brands such as Aston Martin, Burberry, Bushmills Irish Whiskey and Vodafone.

Activities

3. In groups, copy and complete the table below to show the benefits of purchasing products from all over the world (imports) and of selling products from Northern Ireland abroad (exports). One example has been filled in already.

Benefits of global trade for Northern Ireland	
Imports	Exports
Better variety of products	Higher sales – more profit

4. Identify and explain why imports and exports are very important to Northern Ireland.

5. Can Northern Irish-based companies ignore globalisation? Give reasons for your answer.

Key words

exports ▪ global economic changes ▪ globalisation ▪ imports

The implications of the global market for Northern Ireland

Companies that are not originally from Northern Ireland but that manufacture or provide services here operate in the global market. Examples of global companies that have a presence in Northern Ireland include: McDonald's, KFC, HSBC, Starbucks and Citigroup.

Northern Irish-founded companies that manufacture or provide services in other countries include Bushmills Irish Whiskey and Moy Park and these also operate in the global market.

The spider diagram on the right shows some of implications of the global market for Northern Ireland. You need to understand both the benefits and disadvantages of globalisation.

Inward investment
Can attract investment in jobs/community projects

Export opportunities
Can advertise local produce to foreign markets through town information

Fluctuation in money markets
A strong pound (worth more than the euro or dollar) can be good for imports but bad for those trying to export

More competition for local business
Local producers face competition for their products, they can be under-priced by foreign rivals

Educational, community and business links
Twinning projects can encourage and help establish links

More employment
Jobs are needed to sell the products, linguists are needed to communicate

Tourism
New people will come to visit and hopefully spend money in the town

Disadvantages

Benefits

Equality with other countries
We are treated as an important voice when decisions about trade have to be made

Civic pride
People may take more pride in their local area and have a sense of belonging

Benefits

Trade with countries all over the world

Product/ service variety
For example, we have fruit and vegetables all year round from countries throughout the world

Town twinning

Negative publicity
Negative publicity associated with twin may have a bad impact for the twinned town by association

Disadvantages

THE GLOBAL MARKET AND NORTHERN IRELAND

Waste of money
Could be viewed as a waste of public money that does not bring anything to the town

New and advanced technology

Competition

Benefits

Disadvantages

Benefits

Disadvantages

Training
New skills acquired to keep up to date

Efficiency
Learning more efficient methods of business leading to less wastage, less manpower and sharing good practice

Continuous investment needed
Takes a lot of resources and finance

Retraining
Expensive to learn new skills and keep up to date to remain competitive

Increased trade/ employment
Leads to more money in the economy and more jobs

Closure and redundancies
Can result in the loss of jobs (especially those that are no longer in demand – e.g. shipbuilders or textile workers)

Activities

6. The spider diagram on page 114 shows that there are some benefits and disadvantages for Northern Irish-based companies because of globalisation.

   a) On a piece of paper or on a sticky note write down one more benefit and one more disadvantage you can think of.

   b) Get into groups of four and share your ideas. Discuss each idea; hopefully your discussion will lead to other ideas.

   c) Pick one person in the group to feed back to the whole class.

   d) Listen to all the feedback and ask questions if you are not sure.

   e) Record all the benefits and disadvantages.

   f) Complete a 'priority pyramid' for the benefits of globalisation and one for the disadvantages. The benefits and disadvantages that you think are the most important go at the top and the least important at the bottom.

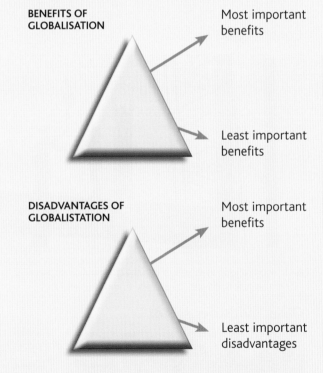

BENEFITS OF GLOBALISATION — Most important benefits / Least important benefits

DISADVANTAGES OF GLOBALISTATION — Most important benefits / Least important disadvantages

7. Use your priority pyramids to help you answer the following:

   a) Give an example of a benefit the **global economy** has for Northern Ireland and explain why it is a benefit.

   b) Give an example of a disadvantage the global economy has for Northern Ireland and explain why it is a disadvantage.

   c) Has the global economy benefited Northern Ireland? Explain your answer.

Key word

global economy

The impact of changing employment patterns on Northern Ireland

Thirty years ago very few companies from Northern Ireland operated abroad and most of the jobs in Northern Ireland were provided by Northern Irish companies. Today the situation is very different. **Employment patterns** have changed, with many people working for multinational companies such as Tesco or for companies that export their goods all over the world such as Bushmills Irish Whiskey.

What are employment patterns?

When someone is employed it usually means that they are in a paid job with a **contract of employment**. Employment patterns refer to the types of jobs we do, who employs us and how many of us are employed at a given time. Over the last 30 years, many changes

have occurred in employment patterns within the UK. These include:

- more women in work
- growth in the number of people employed in the public sector, such as the NHS
- growth in the service industries such as banking, IT and tourism
- decline in manufacturing industries such as shipbuilding
- changing employee and consumer demands.

In Northern Ireland, like elsewhere in the UK, the pattern of employment has changed. The table and graph on page 117 illustrate this for the following different employment sectors.

Manufacturing sector

▲ These are jobs involved in the production of goods such as food, vehicles, pharmaceutical products, engines, machines, etc.

Service sector

▲ These are jobs involved in providing services such as retail staff, teachers, nurses, travel agents, hairdressers, administration staff, etc.

Construction sector

▲ These are jobs involved in constructing buildings, such as architects, bricklayers, labourers, engineers, etc.

Other industries sector

▲ These are any other types of jobs that do not fall into the other categories such as agricultural (farming), fishing, fruit picking, etc.

Year	Manufacturing	Construction	Services	Other industries	Total employed
2003	89,270	36,285	525,800	22,270	673,625
2004	86,390	37,300	539,325	22,690	685,705
2005	84,450	39,415	554,245	21,910	700,020
2006	83,950	42,420	561,935	21,190	709,495
2007	83,705	44,850	573,350	21,185	723,090
2008	82,000	43,410	579,895	21,185	726,490
2009	75,840	36,750	572,565	20,865	706,020

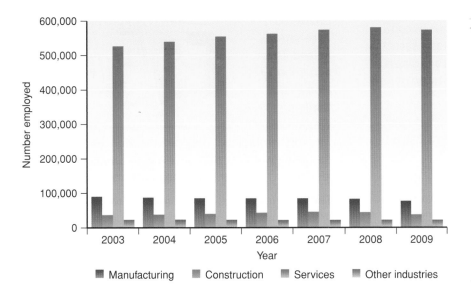

◀ The table and graph illustrate the number of people employed by sector in Northern Ireland from 2003–2009 (Adapted from Department of Enterprise, Trade and Investment (NI) Monthly Labour Market Report, published 12 May 2010)

Activities

1. What do the graph and table tell you about manufacturing jobs in Northern Ireland? Why do you think this is the case?

2. What do the graph and table tell you about service jobs in Northern Ireland? Why do you think this is the case?

3. Why do you think there was a drop in employment figures in 2009?

4. How have employment patterns in Northern Ireland changed from 2003?

5. The Office for National Statistics (www.ons.gov.uk) produces independent information to improve our understanding of the UK's economy and society. Go to its website and:

   • click on 'UK snapshot' in the menu at the top of the screen

   • click on 'labour market' under the brief analysis

   • click the link 'employment' and answer the following questions:

   a) What is the current employment rate?

   b) Has this rate increased or decreased from the previous quarter?

   c) Can you think of any reasons for the change?

Key words

employment patterns ▪ contract of employment

Why have employment patterns changed?

There are many reasons for changing patterns of employment in the UK. These include the introduction of **new technology** requiring new and different skills, and the fact that many companies have moved abroad. The case study below and on page 119 illustrate this.

Case study

Web design

Biznet is an Internet solutions company, founded in 1997 by Adrian Bradley and Daryl Fullerton. It began as a small web-based company that has grown into two independent businesses under the Biznet brand: www.biznetiis.com and www.bizneteis.com. The Biznet story is one that demonstrates a success story in the Internet solutions area. It is a business borne out of a demand for new skills because of new technology.

The Biznet group of companies now employs over 76 full-time staff and has offices in Belfast, Dublin, London, Dubai and Houston, Texas.

The Biznet EIS part of the brand focuses on the delivery of performance management software solutions to the international oil and gas industry. This helps companies such as BP, Noble Energy, Gaz de France and Shell use up-to-date software packages to gather, assess and analyse data that helps them decide if a business decision or process has been worthwhile.

The Biznet IIS part of the brand focuses on many aspects of Internet solutions for businesses. The company works across a wide range of sectors delivering a variety of solutions and services for businesses, enterprises and educational organisations. Some of these include Fáilte Ireland, Good Food Ireland, County Dublin Vocational

Education Committee, Maxol Direct, Dublin Bus, Institute of Chartered Accountants Ireland, Town and Country Homes and the Police Ombudsman for Northern Ireland. They provide services such as designing websites that offer a wide range of online facilities to the client and their customers.

The fast growth and development of this home-grown company demonstrates how the introduction of new technology can mean that technological-based skills are now an essential part of the employment market and will continue to affect employment patterns in Northern Ireland.

'We specialise in web-based business improvement solutions for all organisations.'

Adrian Bradley, Managing Director, biznetIIS

www.biznetiis.com

Activities

6. How does the Biznet case study show the importance of new technologies for employment in Northern Ireland?

7. Why is it important for companies to use new technologies such as websites?

8. Using www.biznetiis.com research the work they have done for one company (this is in the case study part of the website). Find out the following:

   a) What were Biznet IIS asked to do for the company?

   b) How did Biznet IIS achieve the company's request?

   c) How has the company's involvement with Biznet IIS developed their use of technology?

   d) Has the work completed by Biznet IIS enabled the company to become more globalised?

Case study

Dyson

James Dyson first came up with the idea of a bagless vacuum cleaner in 1978 but it was not until fifteen years and 5000 prototypes later that he launched Dyson Limited to produce his design, because no other manufacturer would take it on.

From the 1990s until 2002 Dyson vacuum cleaners were produced in the UK but in 2002 the company decided to move its production to Malaysia. This resulted in the loss of over 800 manufacturing jobs in the UK. The company gave the following reasons for the move:

- Manufacturing is closer to suppliers (many of the parts used to make a Dyson vacuum cleaner are to be found in South East Asia) reducing transportation and environmental costs.
- Competitors copying the bagless technology and selling at a lower price forced the company to try to reduce its overheads and there are lower labour and factory costs in Malaysia.
- It is easier to get planning permission to extend the factory in Malaysia.

Costs

UK worker: £9 per hour
Malaysian worker: £3 per hour
UK office rent: £114 sq m a year
Malaysia office rent: £38 sq m a year

Source: Economist Intelligence Unit and BBC

Although Dyson remains a UK company, its products are now produced outside the UK. The company is the bestselling brand in the US, Europe, Australasia and Russia.

James Dyson had this to say about moving from the UK to Malaysia when interviewed by the *Independent on Sunday* (27 February 2005), 'I would love to still be there [the UK] now, but it simply wasn't possible. If anyone else thinks it is, they are welcome to have a go. But I wasted a lot of money on the factory trying to do it.'

Activity

9. Read the Dyson case study and answer the following questions.

   a) What was the impact of Dyson moving manufacturing to Malaysia on the UK employment market?

   b) Explain the reasons Dyson gave for moving production to Malaysia.

   c) How does the example of Dyson in the case study demonstrate globalisation?

Owing to globalisation many manufacturing companies like Dyson are finding it cheaper to make goods in other countries. Globalisation has also meant that companies like Biznet have become very successful because of the demand for the skills, expertise and knowledge needed by traditional based companies (customers of biznetIIS) to use the new technologies to keep their businesses profitable.

Globalisation has affected working life for us all, whether it is through new technologies, enhanced communication or new job practices such as job sharing or teleworking.

Key word

new technologies

Activities

1. Explain what is meant by the terms emigration and immigration.

2. Why is the global market important for employers and employees in Northern Ireland?

3. Why do you think there has been a global increase in emigration?

4. Why is it important that businesses are aware of and understand the impact of immigration and emigration?

The impact of emigration and immigration on Northern Ireland

When someone moves out of a country it is known as **emigration** and when they move into a country it is known as **immigration**. People who leave their country to live elsewhere are known as emigrants in their own country and immigrants in the country they go to.

Northern Ireland is part of the European Union (EU) and our patterns of employment (the jobs we do and how many jobs there are) are influenced by the EU. We also rely on USA based companies to supply employment. We have to understand that we are part of a global economy and emigration is a part of this. More and more people are moving countries to find work and we in Northern Ireland must become an important player in the global market if we are to grow and survive.

There are lots of reasons for migration in our global society such as: looking for work, moving to a place where your work skills are required, retirement, reuniting of families, emigrants returning to their country of birth.

Immigration

There has always been movement of people from one country to another and Northern Ireland has always experienced both emigration and immigration. The patterns of **migration** for Northern Ireland are more like the Republic of Ireland than the rest of the UK and since the nineteenth century there have traditionally been more emigrants than immigrants. However, in the last ten years there has been a significant growth in immigration into Northern Ireland from countries outside the UK, more so since the enlargement of the EU in 2004.

People from Poland, Romania and the Philippines are just some of the immigrants who have come to Northern Ireland for work. These people bring vital skills with them that help the economy to grow and flourish. Likewise, many people left Northern Ireland to work in Europe, USA and Australia when their skills were required in these countries in the 1970s and 1980s.

Advantages	Disadvantages
More choice of employees for employers	More competition for job vacancies
Migrant workers can fill job vacancies that native workers 'do not want'	Migrant workers may mask skills gaps of natives
Bring cultural diversity to Northern Ireland – language, food, music	Migrants may not stay in Northern Ireland – taking their skills and expertise with them
Can teach natives new ways or different approaches to completing tasks or solving problems	

Advantages and disadvantages of immigration.

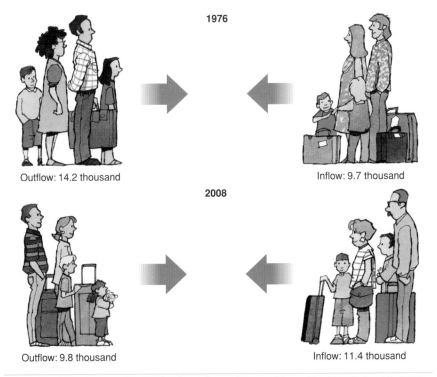

1976

Outflow: 14.2 thousand

Inflow: 9.7 thousand

2008

Outflow: 9.8 thousand

Inflow: 11.4 thousand

Diagram showing the outflow and inflow of people to and from Northern Ireland in 1976 and 2008. It shows that in the 1970s more people left Northern Ireland than those who came to live in Northern Ireland. In 2008 the situation was reversed. This may be because there is more political stability in Northern Ireland than there was in the 1970s.

Activities

5. Copy and complete the following passage using the correct words from those underlined.

> Having *migrant workers* in Northern Ireland means that employers have <u>more/less</u> choice when recruiting. The job market in Northern Ireland may have become <u>more/less</u> competitive because of *migrant workers*. Many *migrant workers* fill job vacancies that natives <u>do/do not</u> want to do.

6. In groups, list the reasons why migrants have decided to come to Northern Ireland.

Why do people come to work in the UK?

Immigration to the UK occurs for many reasons. These can be grouped into PUSH and PULL factors. Push factors are the reasons why immigrants feel the need to leave their country of origin, while pull factors are the reasons immigrants feel drawn towards the UK.

Push factors

- Limited job opportunities in the immigrant's own country – it could be that there is not as much opportunity for career progression.
- High unemployment – it could be that there is a surplus of skills in the immigrant's country of origin.
- Limited opportunities to study – there may be limited opportunities to study as an adult in the immigrant's country of origin.
- To escape from persecution or civil unrest – the country of origin may be involved in civil dispute that could affect work opportunities for the immigrant.

Pull factors

- Higher salaries in the UK – this allows the immigrant to send money back to their country of origin and their family.

- Potential to become self-employed – an immigrant can earn money and gain experience and then utilise the government agencies in the UK to become self-employed.
- Recruitment of employment agencies – UK-based employment agencies may have travelled to the immigrant's country and offered work.
- Better quality of life – the UK may offer an immigrant a better standard of living in terms of housing, education and health care provision.

Key words

immigration ■ emigration ■ migration

121

Patterns of employment for migrant workers in Northern Ireland

Many migrants work in different industries in Northern Ireland, including food processing, construction, engineering, agriculture, hospitality and health care. Workers from different national backgrounds can be found working in any of these industries. However, some patterns are beginning to emerge between nationality and occupation.

For example, there are high levels of Portuguese-speaking and Polish workers in food processing factories in Ballymena, Derry/Londonderry, Coleraine, Dungannon and Portadown. The public and private health care sector in Northern Ireland benefits particularly from nurses and medical practitioners from the Philippines and India. A large number of Lithuanians have also worked on mushroom farms and in other agriculture businesses in Newtownards, Portadown and the border region.

Experiences of migrant workers in Northern Ireland

In 2008 the Department for Employment and Learning decided to find out about the experiences of over 200 migrant workers in Northern Ireland. The research was carried out between May 2008 and January 2009. Migrant workers' experiences were researched through questionnaires and interviews of the migrant workers themselves, their families, their employers and migrant worker support agencies.

The report highlighted the following things:

- The majority of migrant workers in Northern Ireland were young (over 70 per cent aged between 18 and 34).
- The majority of migrant workers in Northern Ireland come from Poland.
- Many of the migrant workers came to Northern Ireland directly from their country of origin.
- The majority of migrant workers came to Northern Ireland because the employment here offered a higher income and an increased quality of life.
- Pay differences between Northern Ireland and the country of origin played a significant role in deciding whether to come or not.
- Many migrant workers in Northern Ireland take on jobs that pay them quite well but they are over-qualified for the posts. Most people are happy with this in the short-term but they will be aiming to get employment in jobs they are qualified for once they have gained a suitable level of English.
- Over 60 per cent of the migrant workers surveyed had never claimed state benefits.
- Many of those surveyed said they found Northern Ireland to be a friendly place, providing a good quality of life in a welcoming atmosphere.

- Some migrants reported that they had been subject to some discrimination with verbal attacks being the most common form of abuse.
- One-third of the migrants surveyed said they wanted to stay in Northern Ireland permanently or in the long-term.

Reuniting families has a great part to play in whether or not migrant workers decide to remain in Northern Ireland.

Why do people leave Northern Ireland?

Northern Irish people who work abroad are migrant workers in other parts of the world. This emigration is part of a global increase in international migration. An indication of the geographical mobility of the population of Northern Ireland is given in a survey carried out by Northern Ireland Life and Times (NILT, 2006) which showed that more than one in four people surveyed said they had lived outside Northern Ireland for more than six months. People choose to leave Northern Ireland for many reasons, some of which are listed below:

- unhappy with the post-conflict situation
- a warmer, drier climate
- attracted to a different culture
- opportunities for children – education, sporting
- better career opportunities – promotion, need for skills
- change of lifestyle and type of living – outdoor activities, beach lifestyle, large city environment
- study in a different location and decide to stay in the location.

Advantages and disadvantages of emigration from Northern Ireland

Emigration can have a negative impact on Northern Ireland's economy if highly trained/educated individuals choose to relocate elsewhere in the world. This leads to a 'brain drain' as they take their skills, knowledge and expertise and put it to work in another area of the world. This means that the Northern Irish economy loses out on the value that could have been added by that individual's skills being used locally.

Another consequence is that the movement of one individual can cause a chain reaction in a family and this can also filter out into a community. This may lead to a situation where an area (usually rural) loses a big proportion of its people as they seek to make a life elsewhere.

Finally, if the emigration is not permanent, it can lead to a situation that is positive for the Northern Irish economy as those who have worked and lived in other areas can then bring their experience and expertise back to Northern Ireland. Hopefully, this can then be put to good use to ensure that good practice is shared about the latest technologies and the most effective methods in business.

Activity

7. List the advantages and disadvantages of emigration for Northern Ireland's economy.

1. Follow the instructions below.

   a) Create a collage using pictures from magazines, newspapers and the Internet to show your use of technologies.

   b) Take the collage home and ask someone aged over 50 to pick out technologies they used when they were your age. Did your older person use any of the same technologies?

   c) What can you conclude from your research?

The impact of the growth of new technologies on Northern Ireland

Each one of you uses different technologies every day. Think about from when you wake in the morning until you go to bed at night. What wakens you? How do you get to school? What technologies do you use in school?

Technology such as computers, mobile phones and the Internet are part of your everyday life and there are probably quite a few you would find it hard to do without! Technology is constantly changing; each year new products come to the market offering different or improved features such as better graphics or faster download times. The technology timeline below shows when some of the technologies we use today were launched.

1976 – Apple I launched – one of the world's first personal home computers

1981 – IBM releases its own affordable personal computer (PC)

1983 – Compact Discs are launched as a new way to store music

1989 – The World Wide Web is invented

1994 – Amazon is launched

1995 – eBay is launched

2001 – Apple launches the iPod

2001 – Wikipedia is launched

2007 – Apple launches the iPhone

2010 – Apple launches the iPad

Technology timeline.

2. **a)** Choose two or three of the items on the timeline and identify ways in which they have influenced our lifestyles.

   b) Can you think of other technologies that have influenced our lifestyles? Find out when they were introduced.

3. List the advantages and disadvantages that new technology can have on our lifestyles. An example has been done for you below.

Advantages	Disadvantages
Easy access to information	Pressure to have the latest piece of technology

Case study

Shopping habits

How many of you have purchased something online? eBay, iTunes or Amazon are just some of the Internet sites that people use to purchase various items on a daily basis. Twenty years ago this was not the case; some used a mail order service but the vast majority of everyday purchases were made in person on the high street or in supermarkets.

Belfast Telegraph

Britons the 'biggest spenders online in Europe'

By Nicky Burridge
Monday, 1 February 2010

Britons are the biggest online spenders in Europe, making nearly a third of all Internet purchases across the continent during 2009, a report showed today.

Consumers in the UK collectively spent an estimated £38 billion online (in 2009), accounting for 30 per cent of total European Internet sales, according to price comparison site Kelkoo.

Despite the recession, online sales grew by 12 per cent in the UK during 2009, with purchases made over the Internet making up 9.5 per cent of all retail sales here.

The report, which was carried out by the Centre for Retail Research, predicts the UK online market will continue to expand during 2010, growing by 12.4 per cent to £42.7bn.

But this growth will be dwarfed by the 19.6 per cent jump the group is expecting across Europe as a whole during the coming year, pushing the total value of sales up to £152.8bn.

The UK is currently the single biggest online market, followed by Germany and France, with these three countries collectively accounting for 70 per cent of Internet sales in Europe.

At the other end of the scale, Poland has the smallest market with sales of only £2.2bn, with Finland and Norway having only slightly bigger markets at £2.3bn and £2.9bn respectively.

Across Europe as a whole, Internet sales accounted for 4.7 per cent of all retail sales, and this figure is expected to increase to 5.5 per cent in 2010.

UK consumers also had the highest average individual online spend during 2009 at £1,102, followed by Denmark at £1,079 and Norway at £979.

Bruce Fair, managing director of Kelkoo UK, said: 'While the retail industry is showing slow signs of recovery, the online shopping sector bucked the trend in 2009 delivering double-digit growth, and is expected to continue to perform strongly in 2010.'

Activities

Read the case study then answer the following questions.

4. How much is it estimated that consumers in the UK spent online in 2009?

5. By what percentage is the UK online market expected to expand in 2010?

6. Which three European countries collectively account for 70 per cent of online sales?

7. Give reasons why you think online purchasing has become so popular in the UK.

8. What effect do you think this expected continued increase in online purchasing habits will have on high street retail outlets?

How has the growth of new technologies affected Northern Ireland?

The growth of new technologies has affected Northern Ireland in a number of ways. It has affected the way we study, the way we work, the way we communicate, the way we shop, the way we spend our leisure time and our future employment opportunities. If companies in Northern Ireland want to remain competitive in the global market they must seek out and use the latest technologies in order to keep one step ahead of the competition. This means that people looking for jobs must be adaptable and willing to learn new skills if they are to be employable.

Jobs that were once considered quite common are now becoming obsolete (no longer needed) in Northern Ireland and the rest of the world because of new technologies. Many jobs can be performed much more quickly and efficiently with the help of technology and, therefore, fewer employees are needed in those roles. Some jobs that are no longer needed or are in decline are:

Travel agents

Many people no longer use the services of a travel agent as the Internet has provided a vehicle for people to plan, book and execute holidays that are tailored to their specific requirements. The contacts or skills of the travel agent are no longer exclusive to the job. Individuals can now purchase flights, accommodation, car hire and insurance using new technology.

Agricultural workers

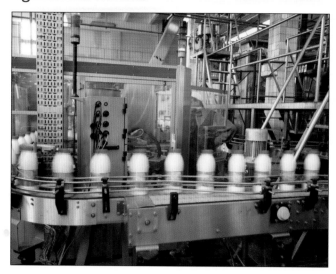

There have been numerous changes in the agricultural industry because of new technology. At one time, milk from cows was extracted by human hands. Due to technological advances the majority of milk is now extracted using machinery. This means that the volume of milk produced is substantially more than it was in the past. However, this also means that the job of 'milk maid' is no longer an employment option.

Typists

Many people who once required a secretary to type and organise files now complete these activities themselves using a computer. This has seen the decline of 'typing pools' (a group of people – usually women – who typed whatever information was required in an organisation/institution).

Telephone operators

A human voice at the end of a phone is increasingly a thing of the past. This job is being replaced by touch-sensitive phones and pre-recorded messages.

Case study

Bombardier Aerospace

Bombardier Aerospace (formerly Short Brothers), based in Belfast and owned by a Canadian company, manufactures components and parts for aeroplanes. In 1987, just before Bombardier bought Short Brothers, there were approximately 8800 people employed. Many of these employees were part of a skilled labour force. However, in 2009 there were approximately 5300 people employed. Some of this reduction can be attributed to the use of technologies such as Computer Aided Manufacturing (CAM) and Computer Aided Engineering (CAE) techniques. The workforce of Bombardier had to retrain and reskill themselves to fully utilise the new technologies to ensure they remained competitive.

Activities

9. Think about how the growth of new technologies has affected Northern Ireland.

   a) Can you think of any other jobs in your area that are in decline?

   b) How much of this decline do you think is due to new technologies being introduced?

10. Look at Bombardier's website (www.bombardier.com) to answer the following questions.

    a) How many countries does Bombardier operate in?

    b) Why do you think it is important that Bombardier employees in Northern Ireland keep up to date with new technologies in the aircraft industry?

Case study

What job should my child do?

The BBC news online reported on a conference held for parents called 'What Job Should My Child Take in a Globalizing Economy?' in Switzerland in 2008. The conference was organised by the World Economic Forum and was attended by parents from all different education and financial backgrounds.

However, the parents were given no clearcut advice about employment guidance for their children as the resounding message from the conference was that no one is sure what the future job market will demand. One participant said, 'The world is developing so rapidly, whichever job you recommend now will be out of date by the time they [children] are out of university.'

All those involved in the discussions agreed that the notion of a lifelong job with the same company was obsolete. They did feel that some jobs would be safe because they depended on 'personal relations' – for example, in industries like health, education and care for the elderly. However, even there one had to differentiate, said one participant. 'The job of a nurse is more secure than that of a radiologist,' she argued, 'because the x-ray image can be sent down a wire

for analysis to any place in the world. Essentially, any service job that can be transported down a wire is insecure.'

It was suggested that parents should not recommend careers but they should encourage their children to develop the right skills to prepare them for this world of uncertainty. 'As parents we have to get our children to globalise as quickly as possible,' said a prominent politician.

The same set of skills that were mentioned again and again were to ensure your children:

- have language skills
- are good communicators
- know how to negotiate
- have people skills
- can understand and appreciate other cultures.

The conference went on to conclude that children need to be encouraged to travel and experience cultures very different from their own in order to be globalised and that the school system has a responsibility to ensure that children and young adults are skilled and equipped to be able to fill the employment needs in the future, whatever they might be.

Activity

11. Read the case study and answer the following questions.

   a) Look at the skills highlighted in the case study 'What job should my child do?' Copy and complete the table below to rate how good you are at each skill.

   b) Use the results in your table to assess how ready you are to enter the globalised employment market and identify what you can do in the future to improve your skills.

Skill	Level Very good/good/poor	Example	How to maintain or improve on skill?
Language skills			
Effective communicator			
Ability to negotiate			
People skills			
Able to appreciate other cultures			

Jobs for the future

An article in the *Guardian* in January 2010 outlined some predictions for the job market in 2020. The article suggested that the following list would be jobs that will be in demand in 2020 because of the impact new technologies will have on society's needs, wants and desires.

Environmental

Jobs to reduce human environmental impact
Jobs to measure the environmental impact of businesses

Renewable Energy

Jobs to generate and sustain renewable fuels such as solar, wind, tidal, hydrogen

Advanced Manufacturing

Product design using mechanical engineering, electronics, controls engineering and computers to make materials for use in new technologies such as self-healing composite materials for use on aircraft, ships and spacecraft

Augmented Reality

Jobs that allow the world of the Internet, 3D and reality to collide in the form of 3D visors connected to bluetooth devices and digital architecture (e.g. marketing on virtual buildings)

Robots and Artificial Intelligence

Jobs where robots can perform tasks more efficiently than humans, such as types of surgery

Jobs where artificial intelligence can predict or give answers faster than humans (e.g. search engines)

Social Services

Jobs that will cater for an ageing population (e.g. nurses, home carers)

Education

Jobs for teachers and lecturers to retrain and reskill the population especially through online courses

Food

Jobs for people involved in organic and locally produced food

Activity

12. Look at the jobs above that might be needed in 2020. Can you think of any other jobs that might be needed because of new technologies and changes in society?

Section 2 Recruitment and selection practices for employment

Learning outcomes

I am learning about:

* the need to pursue lifelong learning to meet changing needs
* the competencies and personal qualities valued by employers, for example:
  * a good standard of literacy and numeracy
  * ICT ability
  * commitment
  * loyalty
  * flexibility

* interview techniques, for example:
  * researching the job and the employer
  * an ability to draw on personal experience.

This section looks at the term 'lifelong learning' and what it means to be adaptable in employment. It explores the need to acknowledge the need for lifelong skills and adaptability. It also examines the advantages and disadvantages associated with lifelong learning and looks at developing an understanding of the terms 'on the job' and 'off the job' training and an appreciation of the relationship between lifelong learning and training.

Lifelong learning

When you are employed by someone you usually have a contract of employment that sets out your terms and conditions such as pay, hours, holidays, the type of job you will do and the leave period you need to give or can expect to receive when your employment ends. You will also usually have a job description which outlines your role and responsibilities in more detail. However, increasingly, because of the fast pace of change in technology, people's duties, responsibilities and ways of carrying out the job often have to change, even though the job title may remain the same.

All those in employment (or looking for employment) should be willing to learn throughout their life. This can be learning about new technologies or adapting skills to suit the type of job they are required to do.

Lifelong learning is the idea that learning new skills is important throughout your life – both during and beyond your school years. Every single day children, young people and adults learn new things. This is because we can always learn something new or a different and better way of doing something we have been doing for a long time.

Think about your ability to read and write. When you were five could you have read and understood this book? Probably not! Your reading skills have continually developed and improved. Likewise, if you look back at things you wrote three years ago you would probably question your style, spelling and construction. You will have improved and you will continue to improve as you continue to learn.

Activities

1. Look at the photographs below – they show just some of the new things a nurse and mechanic might have to learn about and change their working practices as a result of. Choose a different job and make a list of things that you think might change that the employee would have to learn about.

2. Think of five things you have learned in the last 24 hours. Write them down and record beside them where the learning happened.

   a) Did all of your learning happen in school?

   b) Where else can you learn?

3. Do you think you stop learning when you leave school or college? Explain your answer.

4. Do you think that once you get a job, you stop learning? Explain your answer.

new practices

new drugs

new health and safety rules

information about diseases

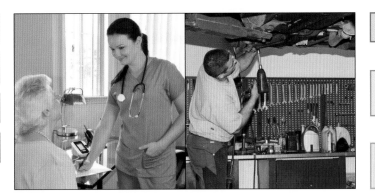

new technologies

new health and safety rules

new models of cars

Activity

5. Both people were asked the question, 'What is a job?' Sample A was written by a seven-year-old, Sample B by a fifteen-year-old.

SAMPLE A

A Jod is nere my Mummy do his Work in a bg Buiding. ste go wen I at scoOl. I got sweets and gams faRm the moey

SAMPLE B

A job is the name given to a role carried out by an indivdual. He/she is usually paid for their time, expertise and or service A job usually involves the person having some responsibilities.

a) What do you notice about Sample A?

b) What are the major differences between Sample A and Sample B?

c) In the space of eight years what learning do you think has occurred?

Key word

lifelong learning

What are some of the lifelong skills needed for employment?

An employer will only employ you if you are knowledgeable and skilled, but they will also expect you to continue to learn and develop existing and new skills. Employers want their employees to be adaptable, flexible and multi-skilled (able to do more than one job).

Below is a list of skills that employers are looking for when they recruit someone (give someone a job), but employers also want their employees to continue to improve and adapt these skills as their business needs change.

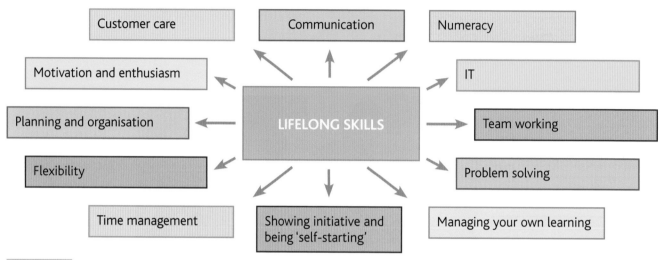

Activity

6. In groups, select two of the skills in the spider diagram above.

   a) Brainstorm what is involved in these skills and think about how they can be learned and improved throughout life.

   b) For each skill write a short explanation that includes:
   - a definition
   - an example
   - how it can be learned throughout life.

   c) Share your explanations with the rest of the class. One example has been given for you on the right.

MOTIVATION AND ENTHUSIASM

Brainstorm ideas – what is this?
Wanting to do something, being eager and keen, being interested, wanting to try your best, giving 100% effort.

What is involved in this and how can it be learned throughout life?

Motivation and enthusiasm is a skill that enables people to complete tasks/ activities using a positive outlook because they want to complete it in the best way they can. Those who are motivated and enthusiastic are keen and eager to do well. When we have a desire to do well then we have the best chance of achievement.

For example, if you are motivated and enthusiastic in your approach to your studies then you will have more chance of being successful. Likewise, you have to be motivated and enthusiastic to compete in a sporting event if you want to achieve the best possible result.

The skill of motivation and enthusiasm is one that you should never stop learning or perfecting in order to succeed and progress in what you do, as employers expect their employees to have a positive attitude.

Is lifelong learning valuable?

You have learned that lifelong learning is required by employers but why do they think it is so important and why are some employees reluctant to get involved in lifelong learning? The table on page 133 shows some advantages and disadvantages to lifelong learning. Can you think of any more?

Advantages	Disadvantages
Allows people to develop the skills they have already	It can be expensive
Lets people develop new skills	It can be time-consuming
Gives people the opportunity to gain more qualifications	May mean people miss out on family time and social engagements
Allows people to meet the needs of an ever-changing employment market	People may be disappointed as may not always lead to promotion
Enables people to gain promotion and maybe a better salary	Can leave the learner feeling tired and stressed
Encourages people to feel more motivated	
Helps people to have more job satisfaction	
Allows people to have higher self-esteem	

Activity

7. Get into groups of four, and then into two pairs (Pair A and Pair B).

   a) Carry out the role plays on the right depending on which pair you are.

   b) Act out your role play to the other members of the group.

   c) A pair from each group could act out their conversation for the whole class.

PAIR A

One person in the pair is the employer and one person is the employee in cartoon 1 below. The employer thinks that lifelong learning is a good idea and is trying to convince the employee that they should be involved in lifelong learning.

PAIR B

One person in the pair is the employer and one person is the employee in cartoon 2 below. The employee thinks that lifelong learning is a good idea and is trying to convince the employer that the business should be involved in lifelong learning.

Cartoon 1

Cartoon 2

What is training?

Training involves learning a new skill or piece of knowledge, usually in order to perform a job or to improve current working practices. Training in the workplace is usually carried out by existing colleagues or by specialist training providers, although some people also carry out independent study in order to become more expert in their job.

New employees usually go through **induction** training when they first start a job. This training helps them to:

- learn about the duties of the job
- meet new colleagues
- see the layout of the building
- learn about the aims and policies of the business.

Many organisations offer opportunities for training throughout the year for all employees. Training is usually divided into two categories: **on the job training** and **off the job training**.

On the job training

This is training that happens while someone is working. It could be when a new employee is watching an established employee perform a task (**job shadowing**), such as operating a machine or watching how someone deals with a customer. What form this takes will depend on the type of job.

Off the job training

This is training that happens when workers are taken away from their place of work to be trained. This may be at a training agency or local college, although some larger businesses also have their own training centres or employ training providers to come into the workplace. Off the job training can take the form of training courses that last a day or more, or self-study. The training can be used to develop more general skills and knowledge that can be used in a variety of situations – for example, management skills or health and safety procedures.

Activities

8. Below are some advantages of on the job and off the job training. Sort them out by copying and completing the table below.

On the job training	Off the job training

a) Cheaper to carry out

g) Employees who are new to a job role become productive as quickly as possible

b) Learn from specialists in that area of work who can provide more in-depth understanding

c) Training is very relevant and practical, dealing with the day-to-day requirements of the job

f) Employees respond better when taken away from the pressures of the working environment

h) Workers may be able to obtain qualifications or certificates

e) Workers are not taken away from jobs so they can still be productive

d) Can more easily deal with groups of workers at the same time

9. What do you think the disadvantages of on the job and off the job training are?

Why is training important in lifelong learning?

Training is important in lifelong learning and an important part of employment because as the needs of society change, the needs of employers change, and employees need to be allowed to develop new skills to meet these changes.

Look at the photographs below. They illustrate how the way we listen to music has changed over the years.

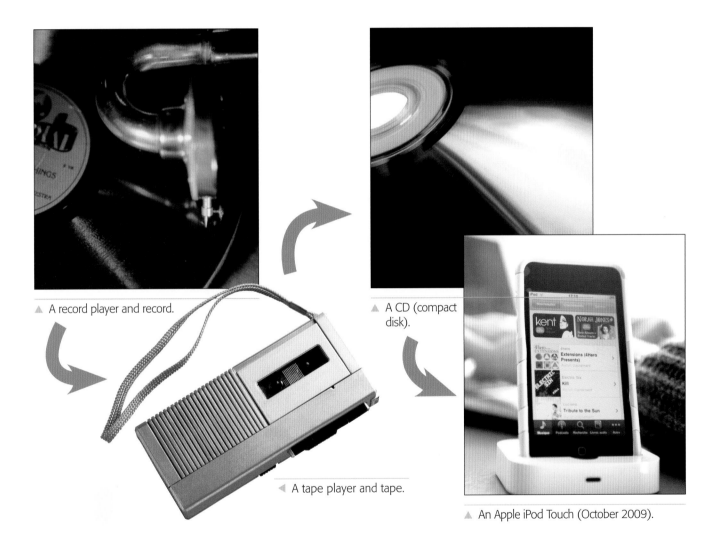

▲ A record player and record.

▲ A CD (compact disk).

◄ A tape player and tape.

▲ An Apple iPod Touch (October 2009).

Each of these changes has meant people involved in the music industry have had to retrain and adapt their skills to provide music in different formats and to meet new challenges such as how to combat piracy.

The example of music above shows the impact that technology has had on the need to change and adapt, but other influences such as the economy also mean people in employment must be adaptable and prepared for change.

Activity

10. Do you know anyone who has changed their job? Why did they do this?

Key words

induction ■ job shadowing ■ on the job training ■ off the job training ■ training

135

How has the 'credit crunch' affected employment?

In 2008 you could not turn on the TV, computer or open a newspaper without learning about the 'credit crunch'. It is a name that has been given to explain how banks and other financial institutions such as credit unions and building societies decided to tighten up on the amount of money they would lend. This meant that it was more difficult for businesses to get credit (money on loan) and for people to get mortgages or loans for cars or house improvements. The financial institutions were not able to lend money because there had been too much money borrowed across the world and it wasn't being paid back, leading them to decide to stop lending so much – they 'crunched' the credit.

As a result, many businesses that relied on credit were left without any money to pay wages and people lost their jobs – they were made **redundant**.

Activities

1. Read the case study on the right and explain what effect you think the credit crunch had on employment in Northern Ireland.

2. What might people who have been made redundant have to do to get new employment?

Case study

Businesses feel bite of credit crunch

The BBC's *Spotlight* programme highlighted the negative effect the credit crunch has had on business in Northern Ireland. The construction industry has suffered greatly as in 2008 it was estimated that 1500 construction jobs were lost, affecting developers, builders, contractors, suppliers and estate agents. This was because the demand for new housing fell dramatically as people wanting to buy homes could no longer get mortgages from financial institutions, which meant the construction workers could not build any new dwellings.

The knock-on effects of this are highlighted by the story of two local businessmen in the Portaferry area. A local fish and chip shop proprietor explained that, since the credit crunch, demand for his fish and chips from construction workers and other customers had decreased hugely and it has left his business in jeopardy. He said 'A lot of small businesses are feeling exactly the same as me. We're wondering can we keep open; we're wondering can we keep going?'

Another Portaferry businessman once ran two successful businesses and employed local people (many of whom ate in the fish and chip shop) in a private development firm (constructing houses) and a supplies shop (builders' merchants). The shop has been forced to close down resulting in the loss of twenty jobs and there have been no properties sold for months. The owner of the businesses said 'We have tried everything and the staff has worked hard, but the work is just not there.'

Stories like this have happened right across Northern Ireland and as unemployment figures increase there is less money to spend on goods and services thus resulting in further job losses.

Key word

redundant

Activity

3. In groups, research how one of the organisations on this page can help people to continue learning, retrain and develop new skills. Explain your findings by using one of the following methods:

a) Make a presentation to the class.

b) Create a 'stall' promoting how the organisation can help people to further learning, retrain and develop new skills. One member of the group stays with the stall while the others move to another stall. The person at the stall promotes the organisation to the other groups. Then, as the groups move to another stall, a new person from the original group stays with the stall to promote it.

> Further and Higher Education Colleges (choose one in your local area – a list of colleges can be found at: www.delni.gov.uk/index/further-and-higher-education/

Careers Service NI www.careersserviceni.com

▲ A part of the Department for Employment and Learning dedicated to informing people about various careers and career paths.

Job Centre www.jobcentreonline.com

▲ A place where those seeking employment can view most job vacancies across the sectors.

EGSA (Educational Guidance Service for Adults) www.egsa.org.uk/

▲ A place for adults seeking information and/or advice about different ways and methods of learning.

The competencies and personal qualities valued by employers

This topic looks at the **skills** and **qualities** that employers want and need in their employees to ensure their businesses are successful. These include good literacy, numeracy and ICT skills, commitment, loyalty and flexibility.

Literacy Skills: the ability to communicate, through talking and listening, reading and writing.

Numeracy Skills: the ability to manipulate numbers and figures and decode diagrams and graphs.

ICT Skills: the ability to use technology such as email and desktop publishing to communicate and distribute information.

Commitment: the ability to stick with a situation or person even when things are difficult.

Loyalty: the ability to believe in and stick up for something or someone when it is being attacked or questioned.

Flexibility: the ability to adapt skills, time and resources to make sure they are being utilised in the best possible way in any given circumstance.

Activity

1. Look at the skills and qualities on the right.

   a) Which ones would an employer want an employee to have, and which ones would they not want? Give reasons for your choices.

   b) What other skills and qualities might an employer be looking for? Produce a list in groups.

   - nervous • worried • lazy • careless • uncaring
   - unpunctual • boisterous • selfish • rude • fun • kind
   - literate • illiterate • numerate • innumerate
   - committed • unreliable • reasonable • thoughtful

Activity

2. Look at the job advertisement, then read the case studies below about two teenagers who want to apply for it. Decide whether Janet or Joshua should get the job. Give reasons for your choice.

Sports Shop For All *is currently recruiting part-time team members. We are looking for very special individuals who have the following skills and qualities to offer:*

- A good standard of literacy (reading, writing, talking and listening)
- A good standard of numeracy (working with numbers, problem solving)
- A good standard in ICT (using technology)
- Commitment (sticks with things)
- Loyalty (keeps his/her word)
- Flexibility (willing to change)

Successful applicants will join a vibrant and fun team where they will be expected to deal with all aspects associated with a busy retail environment.

Application forms and more information are available from **www.SportsShopForAll.co.uk** or by writing to:
Sports Shop For All • 54 Arcade Road • Belfast • BT1

We are an equal opportunities employer

Case study

Janet

Janet is seventeen years of age. She really wants a part-time job while studying in Year 13. She has a grade C in both English and Maths at GCSE.

She has changed her post-16 course choice three times since returning to school. She has been part of the school's football team, choir and drama group but she has only stayed in each for a few weeks.

She spends quite a bit of time on the computer as she has lots of friends on her social networking site. She uses the computer at least twice a day and she always uses her mobile phone to text and update her status profile on her social networking site.

She really wants the job in the sports shop because she wants to get retail experience so she can get a job in a larger shop that doesn't just sell sports clothes. She can also get all of her friends a discount!

She only wants to work on Saturday mornings as she likes hanging out with her friends on Saturday afternoons.

Case study

Joshua

Joshua is sixteen years of age. He really wants a part-time job in a sports shop as he loves every kind of sport and he enjoys working with the public. He is willing to work as much as he can as long as it doesn't interfere with his studies for his GCSEs. He wants to do well at school and he would like to study sport management at university.

He is very involved in clubs and societies at school. He plays in school sports teams and he coaches younger children. He stays behind one day a week in school to help local primary schoolchildren and the junior children in his school with their homework. He helps them to read and demonstrates how to use Moviemaker and PowerPoint on the computer.

Key words

qualities ■ skills

The application process

When **recruiting** new employees, employers are looking for the **PERFECT PERSON** for their job. Depending on the job they might be looking for some with the following characteristics/**competencies**.

PRESENTABLE	**P**ERCEPTIVE
EFFICIENT	**E**NTHUSIASTIC
RELIABLE	**R**ESOURCEFUL
FULL OF ENERGY	**S**TABLE
EDUCATED	**O**RGANISED
CAREFUL	**N**EGOTIATOR
TACTFUL	

Activity

1. Get into pairs or groups.

   a) Pick a job that you have some knowledge of. For this job decide which characteristics are most important for the person employed. You must work together in deciding which characteristics are more important or necessary than the others. You need to write each one on a sticky note or a piece of paper and build a wall. The most important characteristics form the bottom of the wall and then the ones you think are next in importance form the second line and so on. It should look a bit like this.

   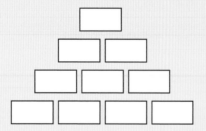

   b) Show the rest of the class your wall, explaining your choices of importance. Make sure you ask each other questions so that each pair or group can justify their choices.

   c) In one minute explain to the rest of the class why it is so important for employers to find the perfect person.

Employers have to recruit people in order to fill their jobs. If a job is empty it is called a job vacancy. The process on how to fill a vacancy is shown in the flowchart below.

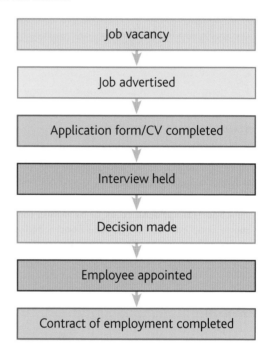

Employers have to advertise vacancies so that people can find out about the availability of jobs. Jobs can be advertised in newspapers, job centres and on Internet sites. Can you think of any more?

The job advert usually tells you about the job and outlines the key competencies, qualities and experience the employer is looking for. Nowadays it often directs you to a website where more information can be found about the vacancy such as a job description and person specification.

A job description sets out the duties of a particular job. A job description for the Sports Shop For All job advertised on page 139 might look like this:

Title: Part-time sales assistant

Duties: Operate till, restock, display stock and assist customers

Responsible to: Supervisor and manager on-duty

A job specification sets out the qualities, skills and desirable features that the company is looking for from a potential employee. A job specification for the Sports Shop For All job might look like this:

	Essential	Desirable
Qualifications		GCSE Maths and English or equivalent
Skills	Good literacy and numeracy and ICT skills	
Experience		Retail Working with the public
Qualities	Loyal Committed Flexible Responsible	Sense of accountability

Activity

2. Explain why you think a business would invest time and money drawing up job descriptions and job specifications for the recruitment process.

Application forms

A job advert also tells you how to apply for the job. This will usually either be through filling in an application form or by sending a CV with a covering letter.

The employer would expect the person applying to demonstrate in their application how they meet some or all of the requirements set out in the job description and specification.

An application form will usually ask you to fill in the following details:

- **Personal details** – name, address, date of birth, nationality.
- **Educational history** – including examination results, schools/universities attended, professional qualifications.
- **Previous employment history** – names of employers, position held, main achievements, pay, reasons for leaving.
- **Suitability and reasons for applying for the job** – a chance for applicants to 'sell themselves'.
- **Names of referees** – often a recent employer or people who know the applicant well (but not family or friends).

Increasingly businesses ask applicants to complete and submit applications online rather than post a paper copy. This use of technology means that applicants can use the spell check facility on their computers and they do not have to worry about illegible handwriting or making too many mistakes.

The advantage to the business is that they save on costs as there is less paper generated and the sorting process can be less time-consuming as the typed word is easier to read and decipher than handwriting. It also means that the application process can be quickened as neither the business nor the potential employee have to rely on postal time.

Key words

competency ▪ recruiting

What is a Curriculum Vitae (CV)?

A CV is a document setting out your details in a clear, brief and interesting manner. As well as showing your previous qualifications and experience, it should show the employer that the skills and qualities you have match the job you are applying for. It can be used instead of or with an application form to get an interview, depending on what the employer asks for.

Remember! Your CV should be modified according to the job you are applying for.

What should be included on a young person's CV?

Personal details

Name, address, telephone number, email address and any other details you wish to include – for example, nationality.

Education, qualifications and training

List your exam passes and mention any courses/training you have done. Remember that accurate dates are very important.

Work experience

- Include any work experience you had whilst at school: part-time and full-time work. Put these in order starting with the last job you had.
- Say where the job was, give the job title and say briefly what you did.
- If you had any gaps – for example, because of unemployment or bringing up a family – include them.
- If you have done any voluntary work add this here.
- Highlight the experience you have had already and be positive!

Skills

This lets the employer see what you have learned from past experiences and what you can bring to the new job – for example, can you speak another language? Have you got a driving licence?

Interests/hobbies

This area can say a lot about the type of person you are. Try to include interests which are relevant to the job you are applying for.

Referees

Always ask a person's permission to use his/her name as a referee. You usually need to supply two names, preferably including one who has known you in a work setting. Give their job titles and full addresses and telephone numbers.

What is a covering letter?

A covering letter is usually included along with a CV. It should encourage the employer to want to know more about the person applying for the job by making them stand out from the rest. The following guidelines should be followed:

- Keep the letter to one A4 page.
- Put your address, telephone and email details at the top right-hand corner and remember to include the date.
- Include the reference number from the job advertisement if there is one.
- If you have a contact name write 'Dear Mr Jones' and end with 'Yours sincerely'; if you don't have a contact name then write 'Dear Sir/Madam' and end with 'Yours faithfully'.
- State what the vacancy is and how you heard about it – for example, 'With reference to your advertisement in the *Belfast Telegraph* on 2 May for …'
- Explain why you want the job and why you think you are suitable for it.
- Include what you are currently doing and how this is relevant to the job you are applying for.
- Sign your name clearly.

Don't forget to enclose your CV with the letter or to attach it if sending it by email.

How is email used in recruitment?

Email is now used for sending and receiving application forms as well as accepting CVs and letters. It is also used in conjunction with or alongside phone calls and traditional posted letters to set up interviews and reject applications both pre- and post-interview.

How are telephones used in recruitment?

Telephones are used in recruitment in the following ways:

- to have an informal chat to see if an application would be appropriate
- to set up the initial interview
- to carry out an interview when the interviewee can't attend in person – usually if the job is in another country (video conferencing can also be used for this)
- to offer the person the job.

Activities

3. The website www.kent.ac.uk/careers/cv/goodbadCV.htm gives examples of good and bad CV techniques. In pairs, use the website to create a poster called 'The DO's and DON'Ts of CVs'. The poster should be displayed to encourage people to write effective and worthwhile CVs.

4. Complete a CV and covering letter for the Sports Shop For All job (see page 139) and email it to your teacher.

What is an interview?

Once an employer has received all the applications, they need to be read and sorted out to decide who to interview. When analysing applications, they are often sieved into three categories.

◼ **Those to reject**
Applicants may be rejected because they do not meet the requirements set out in the job specification such as wrong qualifications or insufficient experience or they may have shown poor literacy skills in their application.

◼ **Those to place on a shortlist**
The shortlist often comprises three to ten of the best applicants who are asked to interview.

◼ **Those to place on a long list**
A business will not normally reject all other candidates immediately but keep some on a long list in case those on the shortlist drop out or do not appear suitable during interview.

Interviewing is the most common form of selection as it is fairly cheap to do. It gives employers the opportunity to meet the applicant face to face and get much more information about what the person is like and how suitable they are for the job. Examples of information that can only be learned from interview and not from a CV or application form are:

◼ Conversational ability – how well an individual can relate to people and different settings.

◼ Natural enthusiasm or manner of the person applying for the job.

◼ Finding out how the applicant reacts under pressure.

◼ Being able to ask questions about details missing from the CV or application form.

At interview the interview panel (people asking the questions) will usually have a list of questions and sometimes have a scoring sheet where they score the applicant's answers according to what they think are the correct answers to the questions.

As part of the interview process employers sometimes ask the applicant to make a presentation and/or complete a test. These tests could either be a generic personality assessment or a more specific competency assessment to see if they are compatible with the requirements of the job. A presentation can allow the applicant to demonstrate their knowledge and communication skills.

Interview techniques

An interview is a great opportunity for a potential employee to show that they are the best person for the job and in order to do this the person being interviewed (the interviewee) should remember to research the job and the employer and use personal experience to highlight their suitability for the job.

You could research the job and employer by talking to current employees of the business (if you know any) or by using the Internet. Things to research might include:

- range of stock carried by the business
- bestsellers
- different types of responsibilities within the business
- busy periods of business
- types of customers that use the business.

Your research should help you to understand the workings of the business and give you some valuable information that you may be able to use in an interview either through answering a question or by asking a question.

TOP TIPS FOR INTERVIEW AND PRESENTATIONS

PREPARATION

✓ Find out about the business and the employer – what does the business do? Is it big/small? Is it a new/old business? Try to get an understanding of the business.

✓ Think about yourself – what skills are you good at? What qualities make you special? What qualities and skills make you employable? What about you would impress an employer?

✓ Find out where the interview is being held – plan your journey. How long will it take? How will you get there? Try to arrive ten minutes before the interview is due to begin to compose yourself.

✓ Think about what you will wear – does the clothing give off the right signals? Does your clothing show that you are respectable? Are the clothes neat, tidy and fresh?

✓ Organise your record of achievement – is everything in order? Is it up to date? Is it clean and not scruffy?

✓ Have a practice interview – what sort of questions will the interviewer ask? How will you answer them? What questions could you ask the interviewer?

✓ Practise your presentation – make sure any electrical equipment is operating properly, have a back-up USB with your presentation/notes.

AT THE INTERVIEW/PRESENTATION

✓ Try not to be too nervous – be pleasant to the receptionist, the interviewer(s) and anyone else you meet, you want to give the right impression – SMILE.

✓ Behave in an appealing way – sit up straight, be polite, be positive, smile, listen carefully, speak clearly, make eye contact.

✓ Answer the questions as best you can – use personal experience to explain a point, show interest, be keen.

✓ Ask a question(s) related to the job/business, show your knowledge.

✓ Keep your presentation to the time limit – have a good closing statement that sums everything up.

Activity

5. Using the information above and your own ideas, design a leaflet that gives advice and guidance to people attending interviews and/or presentations.

Key word

interview technique

Success at interview

Joshua (see page 139) was offered a job in Sports Shop For All after a successful interview. However, before this happened the company checked out his references to investigate his character further. Once the company was satisfied with Joshua's history, character and abilities they then offered him the job by sending him a letter in the post (letter of agreement). This could also have been sent via email, or some companies telephone and then send out a letter of agreement. Joshua decided to accept the job and he then signed his contract of employment and began his training.

However, some people may still want clarification from their prospective employers on salaries, holidays and career progression before they sign their contract and it is after the letter of agreement is received that they will negotiate these issues with their potential employers.

Activities

6. Think of five questions and answers that Joshua may have been asked and answered in his successful interview. Look back at the information on Joshua on page 139 and the information on interviews on pages 144–45 to help.

7. Think about your skills and capabilities and look for a job that you would like to apply for. You can look in newspapers or on the Internet. Below are some sites you could use:

www.jobcentreonline.com
www.nijobs.com
www.nijobfinder.co.uk
www.recruitni.com
www.e4s.co.uk

a) Research the job. Find out as much information about the job and company as you can.

b) Find a blank application form or complete a CV and covering letter for the job of your choice.

CV Links

www.careersserviceni.com/Cultures/en-GB/FindAJob/Advice/Compile+a+CV.htm

Blank application forms

www.docstoc.com/docs/1688067/Blank-Copy-of-a-Job-Application

www.samplewords.com/professional-job-application-form.html

c) In pairs, decide on a topic or scenario that you could use to present as part of your interview. Possible topics or scenarios could include:

- dealing with a difficult customer (working in retail)
- dealing with a medical emergency in the workplace (any type of job involving people)
- planning an event (manager/fundraiser)
- working with outside agencies as part of your job (community worker).

The topic or scenario will depend on the job and the duties and skills involved in it.

d) As an individual prepare a presentation to give to an interview panel (group from your class, or careers teacher and others). Remember when presenting to:

- explain the purpose of your presentation
- talk to your audience (interview panel)
- keep your audience interested
- make the presentation original (different)
- use positive body language (smile, make eye contact, stand straight).

Be prepared to take some questions from the interview panel – think of possible questions and answers.

e) Allow the interview panel to decide if you have got the job by judging your presentation and application form or CV.

f) Instead of a presentation you could do some mock interviews. This would mean researching possible interview questions in pairs (see the links below as a starting point) and then interviewing each other and deciding whether or not you have been successful. You could try to work out a scoring system for the questions you are going to ask (see links below as a starting point). Remember the questions and answers must be suitable for the job and that five questions for the interview are enough.

Help with questions

www.jobinterviewquestions.org/questions/interview-questions.asp

www.interview-advice.co.uk/common-interview-questions.html

Help with scoring interview questions

www.admin.state.mn.us (then search for the 'Sample rating criteria' document)

Section 3 Rights and responsibilities of employers and employees

Learning outcomes

I am learning about:

* the areas in which an employer owes a duty of care to an employee, including: salary, health and safety, career development, compassionate leave, holidays

* the responsibilities that an employee has to an employer, for example: loyalty, honesty, timekeeping, meeting deadlines

* ways in which businesses can become more socially aware, for example by addressing issues of sustainability and climate change.

This section looks at the areas in which an employer has a duty of care to an employee. It looks at the responsibilities an employer has for an employee such as salary, health and safety, career development, compassionate leave and holidays. It explores the responsibilities that an employee has to employers. Finally it examines ways in which businesses can become more socially aware in terms of sustainability and climate change.

What are rights and responsibilities?

Both employers and employees have rights and responsibilities in regards to themselves and each other.

Rights

A right is something a person can expect to receive. An employer has a duty of care (must make sure their employee's rights are provided for and carried out) to employees. These are some rights an employee has:

* to be paid for the work he/she does – receive a salary
* to be safe in work – health and safety
* to have opportunity for promotion – career development/progression
* to have holidays – holiday entitlement
* to be protected from discrimination – equality in gender, race, disability, etc.
* to be shown consideration for personal matters – compassionate leave.

Responsibilities

A responsibility is something we have to do in order to have rights. An employer has the responsibility to make sure the employee's rights are met. The responsibilities for the rights listed previously are:

* pay employees a fair wage on time
* make sure the workplace is safe
* make opportunities available for career development/progression (promotion)
* follow legislation (laws), treat everyone equally
* give a paid holiday entitlement of – usually – 28 days (including bank holidays)
* allow unpaid time for family emergencies.

All of these rights are protected by law as the table on page 149 shows. This means that legislation has been passed by the government to make sure employees are protected. If the laws are not followed then the employer can be prosecuted and sued in court.

Law	Employees' rights	Employers' responsibilities
Equal Pay Act (NI) 1970	Men and women must be paid the same amount if they are doing a job of 'equal value' (same skills, same level of knowledge and same demands), in both part-time and full-time work.	Must ensure that all employees are paid equally if they are doing jobs of 'equal value'.
Sex Discrimination (NI) Order 1976	Men and women must have equal treatment and opportunity in the workplace. This includes areas such as recruitment, promotion, job conditions and pay.	Must ensure that no one is discriminated against because of their gender.
Race Relations (NI) Order (2003)	People of all races, colours, nationalities and ethnic origins must be treated equally in the areas of recruitment, employment and training.	Must ensure that no one is discriminated against because of their race.
Disability Discrimination Act 1995	Able bodied, disabled and some people with mental impairments (depends on the mental impairment) must be given the same opportunities in recruitment and employment.	Must ensure that no one with a disability is discriminated against and employers must make reasonable adjustments to accommodate those employees who are disabled.
Health and Safety at Work (NI) Order (1978)	All employees must be allowed to carry out their work in a safe environment. This includes being provided with any specialist safety equipment that is required.	Must ensure many things, some of which are: • the safe use of articles and substances that could cause harm • provide health and safety training • provide protective clothing and equipment • maintain all equipment • provide a safe working environment.
National Minimum Wage Act (1998)	All employees depending on their age must receive a minimum hourly wage for their work.	Must ensure that employees are paid a minimum hourly wage (depending on their age) as stipulated each year by the government.
Working Time Regulations (NI) order (1998)	This covers things such as holiday entitlement, the maximum hours an employee is expected to work, rest break entitlement, rest periods between working days and nights and Sunday working hours.	Workers over eighteen are generally entitled to: • 20–25 days' holiday per year (not including bank holidays) • twenty minute break if the shift is longer than six hours • work no more than six days out of every seven, or twelve out of every fourteen days • work a maximum of 48 hours per week.
Employment Act (2002)	• Parents of children under six or with a disabled child under eighteen are allowed to ask to work flexibly. • Fathers can have two weeks of paid paternity leave (paid at same rate as statutory maternity pay) within eight weeks of birth or placement of a new child. • Parents adopting a new child will receive the same leave as given for maternity leave (where possible).	• Employers must take any requests for flexible working requests seriously. • Fathers must be allowed to take paternity leave without question. • Make sure employees have worked continuously for at least 26 weeks before the application is made.

Laws that protect employees' rights

Activities

1. Do you think an employee should have other rights than those listed? If so, what would they be?

2. List the associated responsibilities for any other rights you thought of.

3. Design a poster for employees outlining their rights in the workplace.

What is a trade union?

A trade union is an organisation that looks after the interests of employees. A trade union's main concern is to make sure that all employees are receiving their rights and that employers are meeting their responsibilities to staff. They do this by:

- giving advice and information to members about things relating to their employment (holiday pay, sick pay, etc.)
- defending employees' rights and resolving conflict
- negotiating pay and working conditions.

Many employees are a member of a particular trade union. Their choice of trade union will depend on their job, as there are different trade unions for different types of jobs. Some examples are shown in the box below.

> The **NASUWT** is a teacher's union which represents teachers in England, Northern Ireland and Wales.
>
> **UNITE** is Britain's biggest union with two million members in every type of workplace such as the transportation, manufacturing and aviation industries.
>
> **UCATT** is a trade union specialising in the construction industry with 125,000 members spread throughout England, Wales, Scotland and Northern Ireland.
>
> **UNISON** is Britain and Europe's biggest public sector union with more than 1.3 million members. It represents people working in the public services (hospital staff, civil servants, etc).

Why would an employee join a trade union?

There are many benefits to being a member of a trade union:

- An individual does not have to speak to management alone if they have a problem.
- The trade union will be able to answer almost any question relating to an individual's contract of employment.
- The trade union can help members who feel they are being treated unfairly by checking the employer's responsibility and seeing if a breach has been made. They can then advise the member about what to do.
- The trade union try to make sure that there is career progression for employees.
- The trade union will negotiate on behalf of its members for good pay and working conditions.

However, some employees choose not to join a trade union.

Why would an employee not join a trade union?

There can be some drawbacks to being part of a trade union for employees. Some of these are:

- You have to pay to be a member and if you never use the services then this can be seen as a waste of money.
- If you are part of a trade union and the majority of members decide to take industrial action (strike, go slow, etc.), then you have to follow the industrial action too even if you do not want to do it – all actions are done as a united group.
- Some employers do not encourage the membership of trade unions and so some employees will decide not to join one.

What do employers think of trade unions?

Some employers encourage their employees to join a trade union while others don't. This is because there are both advantages and disadvantages to the employer if employees are in a trade union. What are they?

Activity

1. Joe is employed as a fire-fighter and he is thinking about joining a trade union.

   a) Find out which trade union he could join by asking a fire-fighter or searching the Internet (try typing 'fire brigade union in Northern Ireland' into a search engine).

   b) List the reasons he should join the trade union.

   c) List the reasons he should not join the trade union.

   d) What would you do if you were Joe? Justify your answer.

| Can deal with the shop steward (union representative) rather than a number of different employees | ← | **ADVANTAGES TO EMPLOYERS OF EMPLOYEES BEING TRADE UNION MEMBERS** | → | Just need to distribute information to the trade union which then passes it on to their members |

| Can encourage members to go against the company's wishes | ← | **DISADVANTAGES TO EMPLOYERS OF EMPLOYEES BEING TRADE UNION MEMBERS** | → | Trade unions can force employers to increase wage rates and improve other terms and conditions |

Industrial action from the whole staff can result in profit losses for the company

Activity

2. Copy each of the diagrams above and in small groups discuss other advantages and disadvantages from the employer's point of view. Add your suggestions to the diagrams.

The responsibilities that an employee has to an employer

Just as employers have responsibilities to their employees, so employees have responsibilities to their employer, because employers have rights too.

What are employers' rights?

Employers have the right to expect:

- loyalty and commitment
- honesty
- good attendance and punctuality
- that deadlines are met.

What are employees' responsibilities?

An employee has the responsibility to make sure these rights are met. The responsibilities for the rights above are listed below.

Employees have the responsibility to:

- put in 100 per cent effort all the time
- be truthful and trustworthy
- attend work on time, every day
- manage time and look for help when needed.

These acrostics might help you to remember the rights and responsibilities of employers and employees.

Encouraging	**E**ngaged
Motivating	**M**otivated
Pleasant	**P**unctual
Leading	**L**oyal
Open to new ideas	**O**pen to learning new skills
Yearly holidays provided	**Y**ield as much profit through 100% effort
Enterprising	**E**nthusiastic
Realistic	**E**nergised

Activity

1. Think about employers' rights and answer the following questions.
   a) Do you think an employer should have other rights than those listed on the left? If so, what would they be?
   b) List the associated responsibilities for any other rights you thought of.

What happens if employees fail to meet their responsibilities?

If employees fail to meet any of their responsibilities they may be in breach of their contract of employment and they can be disciplined. Disciplinary action will depend on the seriousness of the breach in responsibility.

The action is usually broken down into:

- verbal warning
- written warning (an employee may receive more than one, depending on the employer's policy)
- dismissal.

A less serious breach, such as being late for work on a few occasions, may result in an employer giving a verbal warning to the employee. A more serious breach, such as missing an important deadline, may result in a written warning being presented to the employee.

A very serious breach, such as stealing or receiving a few written warnings, may result in the employee being dismissed.

Activity

2. Divide into pairs and devise a role play situation that demonstrates disciplinary action between an employer and an employee. The degree and nature of the situation is to be decided by you and your partner. Act out your role play for the class.

Rewarding responsible employees

Employees who meet their responsibilities are often rewarded by their employers. These rewards can be broken down into financial and non-financial.

Financial rewards are monetary rewards such as:

- **Bonus** – an extra payment for meeting targets or deadlines.
- **Commission** – an extra payment based on a percentage (usually on the sales made by an employee).
- **Profit-sharing** – employees receive a share of the profits made by the business.

Non-financial rewards are other ways employers thank their staff for meeting their responsibilities. These could include:

- **Job enrichment** – when employees are given interesting, challenging and more complex tasks as a reward. This could be when an employee is allowed to get involved in the whole unit of work rather than individual, separate tasks.
- **Job enlargement** – when employees are given more tasks to do that are similar to the ones they are already completing. It means that employees have more responsibility and have more variety in their work.
- **Empowerment** – when employees are given more authority and encouraged to make decisions regarding their time management and task priority.
- **Recognition/status** – when employers make sure the employee feels appreciated by recognising their hard work and praising the employee, and this can be done through schemes such as 'Employee of the Month'.
- **Consultation** – when employers take time to find out employees' views and are willing to discuss their suggestions.

Activity

3. Place a seat in the middle of the classroom. This is called the hot seat. Three people in the class are asked to take on the following roles for the hot seat:

- an employee who meets all their responsibilities
- an employee who often fails to meet their responsibilities
- the employer of the two employees.

a) The three people in the hot seat should be given time to think about their character as they are going to be asked questions by the rest of the class.

b) Everyone else in the class should think of one question each to ask the three people who will be in the hot seat.

Possible questions might include:

- Why do you think you should be rewarded?
- What are your responsibilities to your employer?
- What is your favourite type of reward and why is this?
- Do you think all employees should be rewarded? Why?
- What rights do you have as an employee?
- What rights do your employees have?
- When would you discipline an employee?
- How would you discipline an employee?

c) When asking the questions to the people in the hot seat vary the questions so that the three 'characters' can give different answers.

d) Once you have finished the hot seat activity write down what you have learned from it. Share your thoughts with the class.

How can businesses become more socially aware?

The term 'socially aware' is a fairly recent addition to business vocabulary. It means that the business will examine its decisions and growth in the light of the environment it operates in, and this can be on both a local and global scale. Many businesses have adopted a Corporate Social Responsibility (CSR) Policy. This covers areas such as monitoring the impact the business has on the well-being of the local and global environment, consumers, employees and other stakeholders (people who have an interest in the business).

What are issues of social awareness?

There are lots of issues that businesses should be concerned with if they are interested in being socially aware. Some of these are:

Reducing waste

Businesses can reduce waste: through creating less packaging; by using email instead of paper; by using both sides of the paper when printing documents; by using fewer toxic cleaning products; by turning off lights and computers when they are not needed; by closing doors (conserving energy).

Reusing

Businesses can reuse: by buying refurbished furniture and equipment; by refilling ink cartridges; by not using plastic cups for drinks; by using scrap paper for telephone messages.

Recycling

Businesses can recycle: by always using recycled products; by making sure the products sold can be recycled; by setting up recycling points and recycling paper and cardboard, plastic, broken machinery and computers; by having appropriate bin facilities for paper, plastic, cardboard and food waste – having the facilities well labelled and with clear instructions; by encouraging employees to use the facilities and rewarding them for doing so.

Mitigating (reducing) greenhouse gas emissions

The three main greenhouse gases are carbon dioxide, methane and nitrous oxide. Carbon dioxide comes from burning fossil fuels such as oil and coal; methane comes from rotting vegetation and landfills; nitrous oxide comes from fertilisers, burning fuels and industrial production. It is believed by many scientists that greenhouse gases have contributed to global warming which causes climate change. They think that in order to slow down or halt climate change governments, businesses and individuals need to reduce the amount of greenhouse gases produced.

Business can reduce greenhouse gas emissions by:
- purchasing energy efficient appliances
- using renewable energy sources such as wind turbines
- reducing electricity and heating demands by, for example, switching everything off at the weekend
- buying goods that will last a long time
- using trains or buses rather than cars when attending meetings, and planning trips more carefully
- recycling and throwing away less rubbish which fills landfills.

Activities

1. What do you think are the three most important issues (from those outlined above) for the following businesses to consider in order to be more socially aware? Explain your choices.
   - a busy supermarket
   - a solicitor's office
   - a large textile factory

2. a) In groups, discuss the effects of being socially aware on business. Your discussion should include:
   - What does it mean to be socially aware?
   - How can businesses be socially aware?
   - The effects of being socially aware for the business and society.

   b) After your group discussion, on your own summarise the main points your group made.

Why should business be concerned about environmental issues?

Businesses are willing to spend time and money trying to lessen their impact on the environment. Why do you think this is the case? The diagram on the right outlines some of the reasons.

The case study below shows that organisations are also socially aware because social issues are of great importance to us in the present and for the future.

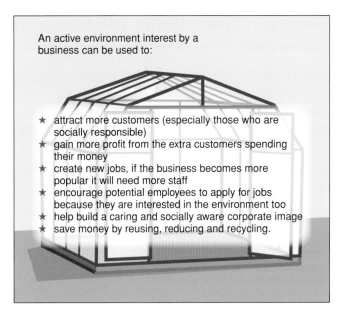

An active environment interest by a business can be used to:

★ attract more customers (especially those who are socially responsible)
★ gain more profit from the extra customers spending their money
★ create new jobs, if the business becomes more popular it will need more staff
★ encourage potential employees to apply for jobs because they are interested in the environment too
★ help build a caring and socially aware corporate image
★ save money by reusing, reducing and recycling.

Activities

3. Read the information contained in the case study below and describe how Belfast City Council is socially responsible when carrying out its work.

4. Identify and explain three things that the inhabitants of Belfast are encouraged to do in order to achieve sustainable development.

5. Identify and explain three ways in which businesses in Belfast can reduce the amount of energy they use.

Case study

Belfast City Council

One of the things Belfast City Council is responsible for is the collecting and disposing of waste generated by businesses and households in the Belfast City Area. In order to do this in a socially responsible way the council must have a concern about the impact this job has on the local and global environment. The council recognises that:

• we all depend on the environment for all our basic needs
• the environment is a source of economic prosperity
• if the council fails to protect the environment, it will not only threaten future generations but will affect lives today.

Belfast City Council believes that a good and healthy environment benefits everyone. They are committed to setting a good example to the people of Belfast by contributing positively to protecting and improving the environment throughout the city by investing time, effort and resources into developing a Sustainable Development Action Plan that identifies key actions to ensure the Council meets its legal obligations for sustainable development.

The Council encourages the residents and workforce of Belfast to help achieve sustainable development in Belfast by making simple changes to their lifestyle. For example:

• reduce the amount of waste created and reuse and recycle materials wherever possible
• choose sustainable forms of transport – for example, by walking, cycling or using public transport
• save energy at home – this helps cut greenhouse gas emissions and reduces the impact of climate change
• help protect the local environment by contributing to the actions outlined in the council's Local Biodiversity Plan. More information can be found at www.belfastcity.gov.uk/biodiversity.

Belfast City Council's Sustainable Development Action Plan can be viewed at:

http://www.belfastcity.gov.uk/parksandopenspaces/localbiodiversityactionplan.pdf

How does climate change affect businesses?

Climate change is the result of global warming. It is predicted that, during the twenty-first century, the average global temperatures will rise by somewhere between 1.4 and 5.8 degrees Celsius. This could result in some places becoming colder, wetter, drier or hotter and susceptible to extreme weather such as hurricanes and droughts. This can have many damaging impacts on businesses. Some are shown in the bullet list.

- Freak weather such as floods can damage property or disrupt the day-to-day running of the business.
- Areas affected by drought will have an impact on businesses that rely on water, either in manufacturing their product or for the health and safety of their employees.
- Poorer air quality brought on by the increase in dangerous gases in the air can lead to air pollution which will have an impact on the health of employees and animals.
- Colder winters and hotter summers will mean higher energy costs for businesses because of heating and air conditioning requirements.

| Source A | Climate change damage may double cost of insurance |

Weather-related problems have been underestimated by scientists

INSURANCE companies are set to raise their estimates for future premiums because of the effects of climate change.

Firms that operate in areas where floods and storms cause a growing amount of damage are likely to see the cost of cover rise by as much as 100 per cent in the next ten years.

The findings by the Association of British Insurers (ABI) believe that the consequences of changes in weather patterns have been underestimated.

A report to be published by the ABI this year argues that previous predictions of climate change damage made in 2005 are too low. Swenja Surminski at the ABI said, 'Climate change is likely to have a more severe impact on the future price, affordability and availability of insurance coverage.'

In Europe, the costliest natural catastrophe was Emma, a winter storm that crossed large parts of Europe with wind speeds of up to 95mph, causing insured losses of $1.5 billion and overall losses of $2 billion.

As the impact of climate change on weather patterns becomes clearer, many companies could start to feel the effects. Matthew Grimwade of Aon, an insurance broker and risk-assessment firm, said, 'We are already seeing rates for natural disasters increasing by about ten per cent, and prices will probably increase more than that by the end of this year.'

The inability to afford or secure an insurance policy for a particular property – be it an office building on the coast of Britain or a manufacturing plant in Asia – poses a number of problems for businesses. It could result in companies shifting their assets to safer locations that are less prone to climatic disasters and it could lead to shifts of employment and economic growth.

There are also likely to be financial implications for governments. A forthcoming report by the International Institute for Applied Systems Analysis, funded by the European Commission, will show that the EU Solidarity Fund, which is worth €1 billion and is supposed to cover 'uninsurable risk' for government-owned infrastructure such as roads and bridges, is not enough to cover the damage caused by the more frequent storms and flooding that are expected.

According to Reinhard Mechler, one of the report's researchers, annual losses from floods alone could rise to as much as €1.2 billion by 2030. 'With a worsening climate an increase in fund resources is needed,' said Mechler.

Adapted from an article in *The Sunday Times* by Tricia Holly Davies, 22 March 2009

What is inner-city renewal?

Another way in which businesses can become more socially aware is by being involved in inner-city renewal projects. Inner-city renewal is where a neglected area within a city is given government grants and funding to be improved through new facilities such as shops, schools, hospitals, leisure centres, etc. The facilities might not always necessarily be new, they could also be refurbished. The case study on Laganside, Belfast on pages 158–59 is a good example of inner-city renewal.

How can inner-city renewal affect employment?

At first you might think that this sort of regeneration could only be a positive thing for employment and on one level it is – new businesses such as supermarkets provide jobs. On the other hand, new businesses have an impact on smaller, already existing businesses that usually struggle to compete with the low cost pricing, huge range and unlimited free parking that can be offered by the newer, bigger, brighter stores.

It is estimated that 2000 corner shops are closing a year and by 2015 they will be completely gone. This can directly be attributed to large supermarkets where three-quarters of the UK's groceries are purchased.

The loss of the corner shop in cities and towns has had a knock-on effect on community relations as it provided employment for local people and was a place where people from the community met, exchanged stories and spent money. Although supermarkets do still employ local people, many people argue that there is not the same sense of community generated by a supermarket. It is also thought that the demise of the corner shop and other local businesses will have a devastating effect on the health of the population's low earners and the elderly as it could lead to a lack of food shops and services in rural and poor areas which are viewed as unprofitable by large retailers.

Activity

6. Read Source A. In groups, discuss the impact climate change and insurance may have on businesses. Present the findings of your discussion to the class using a flip chart or the whiteboard.

Activities

7. What is inner-city renewal?

8. Describe an example of inner-city renewal.

9. Explain how the opening of a new supermarket in a town centre is good for employment.

10. Describe how a local food shop can be affected by the opening of a new supermarket close by.

11. Evaluate the impact that inner-city renewal can have on employment.

Case study

Belfast Laganside

The Laganside Corporation was established in 1989 to undertake the social and economic regeneration of a designated area of land along and around the River Lagan in Belfast. It was an area set in the heart of the city that was derelict and under-used with a heavily polluted river. The Corporation closed in 2007 after having successfully completed and met its Mission Statement:

'Contributing to the revitalisation of Belfast and Northern Ireland by transforming Laganside to be attractive, accessible and sustainable, recognised as a place of opportunity for all.'

The Laganside Corporation was established by the government and it worked with Belfast City Council and Belfast Harbour Commissioners to regenerate the social and economic life of the area. It is a successful example of inner-city renewal as for every £1 spent by the Corporation over £5 was invested by others. It brought and continues to bring jobs, economic growth, tourism and a sense of pride to the City of Belfast.

As a result of Laganside, Belfast has rediscovered its waterfront and the riverside has become a focus for business, leisure and cultural activity. The River Lagan is now viewed as a major asset, an exciting place to work, live and play. The following timeline highlights its achievements and successes and shows some of the landmarks:

1989
Laganside Corporation established.

1994
Opening of the Lagan Weir. The River Lagan holds water events such as jet skiing, rowing and there are over 4km of pathways for pedestrians and cyclists.

1997
Waterfront Hall opens in Lanyon Place.

1998
5 Star Hilton Hotel opened.

1999
The renovated St George's Market opened: Ireland's oldest covered market, selling fresh produce and offering space for smaller concert venues.

Case study *continued*

2000

Odyssey Arena opened: holds leisure events from concerts to bowling, from interactive science activities to the cinema.

2001

1800 jobs in Halifax Internet Banking Centre created.

Writers Square refurbished.

2002

Waterfront Hall named as top conference centre in Europe.

Northbrook Technology move into offices at Lanyon Place.

2005

Custom House Square opened: an outdoor space for festivals and events.

2006

St Anne's Square developed, part of the Cathedral Quarter: a collection of cobbled streets and listed buildings with shops, bars and restaurants.

2007

Laganside Corporation closed with over £1 billion of investment generated within the area.

Activities

12. In pairs, using the information given in the case study and information from the website www.laganside.com, put together a presentation about Laganside. The purpose of the presentation is to demonstrate how Laganside is a good example of inner-city renewal and you will be presenting to your classmates.

    When preparing your presentation consider the following questions:

    • Why was the Laganside Corporation set up?
    • Who has benefited from Laganside?
    • How has Laganside added to Belfast and Northern Ireland?
    • Have there been any drawbacks associated with Laganside?

13. You can try creating your own urban renewal project at Laganside by going to:

    www.bbc.co.uk/northernireland/schools/11_16/ks3geography/swf/settlement/casestudy1.shtml

Section 4 Issues of self-employment and sources of support

Learning outcomes

I am learning about:

* the advantages and disadvantages of being self-employed, for example opportunities and risks
* the support provided by the following agencies:
  * The Department of Employment and Learning (DEL)
  * The Department of Enterprise, Trade and Investment (DETI)
  * Invest Northern Ireland
  * Enterprise Northern Ireland
  * The Prince's Trust.

This section looks at the advantages and disadvantages of being self-employed. It explores the opportunities and risks that may arise from self-employment. It also investigates the different agencies that can offer support to those in self-employment or those wishing to be self-employed.

The advantages and disadvantages of being self-employed

What is self-employment?

'**Self-employment**' is the term used to describe when people work for themselves. They are their own boss. They are often both the employer and employee. People become self-employed to set up and build a business and make money – often referred to as '**entrepreneurs**'. Others are self-employed because that is the nature of their work but they are not necessarily entrepreneurs, such as self-employed taxi drivers, supply teachers and freelance journalists.

What is an entrepreneur?

An entrepreneur is the name given to a person who has the will and desire to work for him/herself and set up a business with all the risk that it entails. Entrepreneurs have an idea or a vision and turn it into an actual business, sometimes with help from various support agencies.

Famous entrepreneurs include:

* Steve Wozniak – founder of Apple Computers
* Bill Gates – founder of Microsoft
* Russell Simmons – founder of Def Jam Records
* Duncan Bannatyne – founder of Bannatyne's Fitness Ltd (also one of the 'dragons' on the BBC televison programme *Dragon's Den*)
* Coco Chanel – founder of Chanel
* Oprah Winfrey – founder of Harpo Productions
* Stelios Haji-Ioannou – founder of easyJet

Do you know any entrepreneurs? What do they do?

Case study

Duncan Bannatyne

This former king of the '99' made money from an ice cream van before moving on to nursing homes and health clubs.

Duncan Bannatyne was born in Glasgow on 2 February 1949. He left school at fifteen with no formal qualifications and he has said that he was easily distracted in school by the thought of the money he was making from his paper round. He joined the navy and trained as a mechanic.

A poverty-stricken childhood steeled Duncan's drive to make his fortune from an early age. After his naval career, which included a spell in military prison, Duncan drifted from job to job ending up in Jersey. It was here that he made the decision to turn his life around.

He began his entrepreneurial life by trading in cars, but it was with an ice cream van purchased for £450 that he changed the course of his life. With 'Duncan's Super Ices', he set out to become the King of the '99' and eventually sold the business for £28,000, founding a nursing home business on the proceeds.

He sold his nursing home business for £46 million in 1996. During the last ten years he has expanded into health clubs with the Bannatyne's chain to his name, and also owns bars, hotels and property. Bannatyne's is now the largest independent chain of health clubs in the UK. Duncan's latest venture is Bannatyne's Sensory Spa, a chain of luxury health and well-being spas.

Quoted on 'The Sunday Times 2009 Rich List' as having wealth to the tune of £320m, Duncan holds an OBE and was recently awarded an honorary Doctor of Science (DSc) from Glasgow Caledonian University for services to business and charity and an honorary Doctor of Business (DBA) from the University of Teesside.

Over 30 charities have benefited from Duncan's involvement and he has recently launched the Bannatyne Charitable Trust to support worthwhile causes.

As a key member of the BBC's *Dragon's Den* programme from 2005, he has agreed investments in the Den that total £1,150,000 across seventeen businesses. This means that he is encouraging other entrepreneurs to realise their dream as well as attempting to make more profit for himself.

www.bbc.co.uk/dragonsden

Activity

1. Read the case study above about Duncan Bannatyne.

   a) Use the case study to compile a profile of Duncan Bannatyne. This should include some personal information (name, date of birth, educational background, etc.) and business information (how he started in business, business success and possible failures).

   b) Now compile a profile of one of the other entrepreneurs listed in the box on page 160 or another entrepreneur you know and present your profile to the class. A useful website you could use for your research is www. topbusinessentrepreneurs.com

   c) Are there any similarities between Duncan Bannatyne's profile and the profile of the entrepreneurs you and your classmates have chosen? If so, what are they?

Key words

entrepreneur ■ self-employment

Setting up a business

Entrepreneurs will usually start their business venture with a new idea or they will adapt an idea that already exists and try to improve it. In order to start a business entrepreneurs have to:

1) Come up with an idea for a product or service.
2) Research whether there is a need for their product or service.
3) Think about how to provide the product or service.
4) Make sure their customers know about the product or service.
5) Organise finance in order to achieve all this.
6) Put accounting procedures in place.

To be able to do this successfully they may need some help and support as they have to research, **design** and **market** the product or service. This is why many entrepreneurs go to specialist agencies for advice and support (see pages 166–68).

Case study

Innocent Drinks

The Innocent Drinks brand was founded by three budding entrepreneurs in 1999. They began the business with £500 of fruit, a smoothie machine, some smoothie recipes and a customer base of a musical festival in London. They decided to conduct some fun research by asking the customers to place their empty smoothie bottles in one of two bins labelled **YES** and **NO**. By the end of the day the YES bin was overflowing indicating that the customers thought the three should give up their jobs and start a smoothie-making business! The three managed to secure an investor and they set up the business after having conducted some more thorough market research.

They set about creating a brand identity and distinctive and innovative designs to house the smoothies. They have since widened their portfoilio to include monthly smoothies as well as seasonal ones to cater for their market (customer base).

Activity

2. After reading the case study about Innocent Drinks answer these questions.

   a) Why would an entrepreneur need to carry out research?

   b) What type of research would an entrepreneur need to carry out?

   c) Why do you think getting the correct design for a product or correct service is so important?

   d) What sort of things would an entrepreneur have to consider when thinking about design?

   e) What does it mean to market a product or service?

   f) How would an entrepreneur go about marketing their idea?

Key words

design ■ market

Where can entrepreneurs find money for a business?

A business is funded by different sources of finance in order to start it up. Successful entrepreneurs usually use a combination of the sources of finance to fund their business venture so that the financial risk is spread. They try to be flexible in their approach to investors and with the terms of payback. Some of the sources of finance include:

- personal savings
- sale of an asset (house, car)
- overdraft (short-term loan from a bank)
- bank loan
- credit cards
- investors (people who put money into the business for a share of the profits or company)
- government assistance (see pages 166–67).

PLANNING

- Think through ideas, look at both the risks and rewards of the idea.
- Think about future problems that might arise and decide how they can be dealt with.
- Be prepared for changes and problems to arise and have plans to solve them.
- Allow time and thought for creativity.
- Research as much as possible.
- Be willing to try different things.

DECISION MAKING

- Trust in the decisions taken.
- Be able to make decisions alone.
- Know when a bad decision has been made and try to fix it.
- Be ready to make quick decisions, sometimes relying on 'gut feeling'.
- Always be responsible for your decisions.

What does it take to be an entrepreneur?

PLANNING
LEADERSHIP
DECISION MAKING
CONNECT IDEAS

LEADERSHIP

- Be willing to take risks and lead by example.
- Be able to manage time, people and investors.
- Use persuasion to encourage people to do what you want.
- Make good decisions even under pressure.
- Use all the information available to make judgements.
- Remain focused even when feeling confused.
- Show commitment and dedication.
- Be able to multitask (do more than one thing).
- Be confident about ideas.
- Be willing to make sacrifices.

CONNECT IDEAS

- Realise that all decisions will have knock-on effects.
- Understand the possible outcomes of decisions.
- Be able to see everything – 'The Big Picture'.
- Realise when something isn't working.
- Not being afraid to stop or change something if it isn't working.

Activities

3. In groups, use as many letters as you can from the alphabet to describe an entrepreneur. For example:

   Astute • **B**elievable • **C**onvincing

4. Now draw a pyramid and place the words where you think they should go. The most important words go at the apex (top) and the ones you feel are less important go at the bottom. This is called a 'priority pyramid'.

5. Underneath your priority pyramid justify some of your choices in a short report. For example:

   I think it is important for an entrepreneur to be convincing because he/she needs to persuade other people to invest in his/her business.

What are the advantages of owning your own business?

The main advantages of owning your own business can be broken down into financial and non-financial as shown.

FINANCIAL

Profits

Money to reinvest

Growing value of the business

NON-FINANCIAL

Satisfaction

Control

Contribution

The financial rewards for being self-employed can be very appealing to entrepreneurs, as many can make lots of money from their businesses. Successful entrepreneurs are often rewarded by being able to afford a high quality lifestyle which may include numerous luxury properties, designer clothes and extravagant holidays. They may also be able to invest some of their money into other businesses where they may be financially rewarded for their investment without having to actually work in the business.

The non-financial rewards for being self-employed are just as appealing to entrepreneurs. These can include: a sense of satisfaction, making a successful business, being in control, employing people, getting good feedback from customers and not having to answer to anyone else.

What are the risks/disadvantages of being self-employed?

There are many risks and disadvantages of being self-employed. A risk is the potential of something going wrong and losing out on money, time or effort. A risk can either go well or fail. When a risk fails the entrepreneur may lose money, have to pay back money borrowed, have difficulty finding a job and have low self-esteem because of the failure.

Business failures are quite common and it is often difficult to know if a business will be successful or not. Some reasons businesses fail include:

- there is lots of competition
- poor cash flow (money in the business)
- an underestimation of the time and effort needed to be self-employed
- not enough customer demand
- poor economic climate
- poor market research
- growing too quickly and not being able to manage the growth.

Case study

Weeping Woolies

The closure of Woolworths in 2008 stunned many high street customers as they believed that Woolworths was one of those stores that would always be around. Opened in 1909 in Liverpool as a shop selling low-priced mass produced items it quickly became successful and, as the decades rolled by, a high street favourite.

Customers would visit Woolworths on a regular basis to purchase entertainment (music, DVDs), homeware (hardware, kitchenware and furniture), children's toys and clothing and confectionery (sweets). However, it was the variety of products for sale that many believe led to the demise of Woolworths. For example, at one point, they had over 40 types of pencil cases for sale in the vast majority of their 800 stores across the UK. This combined with falling sales, stiff competition from the likes of Tesco, a struggling global and local economy and a poor cash flow situation (more money going out than coming in), as well as indecisive and unfocused management and vision all added to the collapse of Woolworths.

Activities

6. Look back at the case study on Duncan Bannatyne on page 161. Explain at least one financial and one non-financial advantage he has had as a result of being a self-employed entrepreneur.

7. In groups of three, have a discussion about the topic 'Avoiding business failure'. Each person in the group should have a role: leader, scribe, presenter. Your discussion should cover the following points:

    a) the reasons why a business can fail

    b) the steps an entrepreneur needs to take to avoid failure

    c) an example of a business that failed and how you think the failure could have been avoided.

8. Present your discussion findings to the rest of the class.

9. Copy and complete the table below. The first example has been done for you.

10. How important do you think self-employment and entrepreneurs are for our society and economy? Why do you think this?

    a) Write down an answer to this question on a piece of paper. When everyone has completed their answer you should stand up and walk around the classroom explaining your answer to other pupils. Try to find someone who has a different point of view or different thoughts from you. Try to persuade them that your answer is valid and reasonable.

    b) List feedback reasons why self-employment and entrepreneurs are important in our society and economy on the board. Those pupils who have changed their original thoughts should explain why they have changed their minds.

Advantages of being self-employed	Disadvantages of being self-employed
Make money	Risk of losing money

Support provided for self-employment

Many people who are self-employed or who want to become self-employed get a lot of support from their family and friends. This can be financial support and/or emotional support. However, other specialist support is usually needed if a self-employment venture is to be successful; this can only be provided by designated agencies that specialise in offering advice and assistance to self-employed people.

Agencies that provide support to self-employed

There are many different designated agencies that can help support self-employed people. Some of the agencies are run by the government and some are Non-Governmental Organisations (NGOs).

The agencies you need to know about are:

- Department for Employment and Learning (DEL)
- Department of Enterprise, Trade and Investment (DETI)
- The Prince's Trust
- Invest Northern Ireland (Invest NI)
- Enterprise Northern Ireland.

Each one of these agencies can be useful for self-employed people. The tables below and on page 167 tell you more about each one of them.

Agency	Role	Support provided	How?	Examples of assistance	Websites
DEL	Helps people to get new skills and provides guidance to those who want to be self-employed	• 'Steps to Work Programme' for those who are 18+ (or 16+ and a lone parent) and unemployed • Graduate Acceleration Programme (GAP)	Opportunities to retrain, get qualifications and work experience under the guidance of an adviser	• Work placements • Qualifications • Personal adviser	www.delni.gov.uk
DETI	Helps to decide and deliver government policy on areas such as Tourism, Social Economy and Enterprise	Mostly through Invest NI (see page 167) but can offer guidance for self-employed people in various different areas	Guidance on areas around: • Tourism • Innovation (new ideas) • Energy • Global markets • Health and Safety	• A place to go if you need information on any of the areas listed to the left • It has policies and statistics that entrepreneurs may find useful when researching or conducting business.	www.detini.gov.uk
The Prince's Trust	Helps young people aged 18–30 who are unemployed to start up in business	Advice on: • Employment options that are available • Business training • Business planning • Funding • Guidance from a mentor	Downloadable guides with help in the following areas: • Business planning • Finding premises • Sales and marketing • Managing finances • Legalities • Taxation • Business behaviour	• 24-hour helpline • Virtual office space • Online accounting system • Web designing • Town and country market opportunities to sell products or services • Money grants	www.princes-trust.org.uk

Activity

1. Match the business needs a)–d) below with the agency (in the tables on pages 166–67) that could help.

   a) A local shopkeeper who wants to expand his premises but is unsure about applying for planning permission.

   b) An unemployed twenty-year-old who has a great idea for a business.

   c) A furniture manufacturer who wants to start exporting his products to the USA and Europe.

   d) An unemployed person wanting to retrain and get qualifications in order to be able to set up in business.

Agency	Role	Support provided	How?	Examples of assistance	Websites
Invest NI	Part of DETNI – gives advice and assistance to new and existing businesses on starting up or growing their business domestically or internationally. Attracts new business to NI	'Go For It' programme and 'Growth' programme offer advice on exporting and global trading and encourage foreign investment to set up in NI	• Meetings, workshops and training seminars (on finance, planning, IT, marketing, design, etc.) for entrepreneurs with ideas • Mentoring support from experts • 'Business Clinics' where problems can be discussed and hopefully solved	• Personal Business advisors • Training and workshops • One-to-one mentoring • Networking opportunities • Online support • Support to develop business plans • Offers grants • Organises international trade fairs	www.investni.com www.nibusinessinfo.co.uk
Enterprise NI	Represents the Local Enterprise Agencies in NI. These are independent, local, not-for-profit companies that try to help support small business development and encourage economic development activity in NI	• Representation of the interests of Local Enterprise Agencies with government agencies, private companies and NGOs working in enterprise and economic development • Provides services for small businesses such as funding and information	• Guidance on grants and initiatives available to small businesses • Professional advice from experienced business people • Advice on programmes available to help businesses and entrepreneurs grow and develop	• Help with finding financial assistance in a particular area. • Help with finding business accommodation • Help with new technologies • Help when using programmes such as 'Go For It' (Invest NI)	Local Enterprise Agency Map can be found at www.enterpriseni.com

How do self-employed people access support and advice?

As you can see there are lots of agencies that are willing to help and advise on self-employment. Below is a case study about how one business received help from Invest NI.

Case study

Monkey Business

When Debbie Chestnutt decided to set up Monkey Business, a children's indoor play area, she realised that she would have to borrow a substantial amount of money. Finding the funding was more difficult than she first imagined but she stuck with it and found the finance she needed. Debbie knew she needed to prepare very detailed costings. When asked  about this she explained, 'I signed up for Invest Northern Ireland's "Go For It" business programme, which provides training and expert advice to anyone thinking of starting a business. As part of the programme we had to prepare a business plan and financial projections.'

'I had no idea how much it would cost to kit out premises and buy specialist equipment. So I visited a couple of similar businesses to find out. I was shocked when I realised how much money I'd need to set up the play area. The play frames alone cost over £80,000 and on top of that I needed to spend around £40,000 on the premises, just on basics like electrics.'

'I prepared a day-by-day cash flow statement. It was extremely detailed. Having done that, I was more determined than ever to go ahead.'

With the preparation and forecasts completed Debbie now had to look for the initial funding. She explains here how she went about this. 'With my business plan and detailed costings I approached the bank for a loan. The bank manager practically laughed at me. He thought my idea wasn't viable, but I'd researched it and I knew it was.'

Case study *continued*

She goes on to explain how this did not put her off. 'Then I heard about a lease company in England that had funded similar businesses. I spoke to them through a broker and without any problem they lent me the money. It's a five-year loan secured against my house. With that and a bit of my own money I was able to go ahead.'

Debbie explored further opportunities for financial support as she explains, 'I knew there were grants available from various sources like the lottery, schemes funded through European monies and so on. However, I was unlucky. When I investigated these I found I'd missed the deadline for applications for some of them and was ineligible for others.'

Debbie explains how she received assistance from other sources as well. 'Monkey Business is near the Michelin Tyre manufacturing plant in Ballymena. Since Michelin is a multinational company that actively supports the local community, I decided to approach them to sponsor our t-shirts. When I did, they suggested I apply for a loan through the Michelin Development fund. The application involved a lot of form filling. I had to provide a business plan and financial projections and stand up to them being challenged. However, I got a loan on very good terms so it was all worthwhile.'

When Debbie was asked what she would do differently she replied, 'I'd look around a bit more for my initial funding, to get the best terms. I was so worried about not getting a loan that I rushed into the first one that came along.' She has these top tips for anyone trying to start up.

Debbie's top tips:

- Prepare very detailed and complete financial projections.
- Explore all available sources of funding to supplement your initial financing source.
- Look around for the best deal you can get on financing.

www.nibusinessinfo.co.uk

Activities

2. How did Invest NI help and support Debbie?

3. What other ways could Invest NI have helped (see page 167)?

4. Which of the other agencies (see page 166–67) could have helped Debbie and how?

5. In groups, imagine that you are starting up a new business. This is your first time being self-employed and you are unsure what steps you need to take.

   a) Decide what the business will be; it could be a new innovation or an already established product or service (e.g. plumber, gardener, alternative therapist, mechanic, hairdresser, designer, retailer, dog groomer, bed and breakfast owner, childminder ... the list is endless!).

   b) Decide if your business is going to employ people or if it will be a sole enterprise (working alone).

   c) Put together a presentation using ICT about which agencies you will go to for specialist help in order to research, design and market your product or service effectively.

Glossary

Glossary for Unit 1 Local and Global Citizenship

absolute poverty where people do not have the basic essentials such as food and shelter which they need to survive

Apartheid the system of political racial segregation in South Africa where the white minority ruled over the non-white majority. Rights of the non-white majority were limited and there was widespread inequality and discrimination

bi-cultural a society where there are only two cultural groups

constituency a voting area or region

democracy a political system where people can vote and have a say in how their country is run

devolution when legislative powers are passed from a central government, e.g. legislative powers being passed from Westminster to a regional government (Northern Ireland Assembly)

devolved government a government with devolved (handed down) legislative powers

discrimination to treat someone unfairly because of the group they belong to

diversity differences within a group or community

ethnic minority a cultural group which is not in the majority in a society. In Northern Ireland the largest ethnic minorities are from the Chinese, Indian, Pakistani, Polish, and Eastern European communities

European Convention on Human Rights (ECHR) introduced in 1953 and inspired by the UDHR. The governments who signed it have a legal obligation to make sure that their citizens enjoy the rights laid down in the treaty

Executive Committee the group of departments which make up the Northern Ireland Assembly. Each department is run by a government Minister who is an elected member of the Northern Ireland Assembly

Good Friday Agreement a political deal which aimed to produce lasting peace in Northern Ireland following the IRA ceasefire of 1994. It was signed in 1998 following multi-party talks and contained proposals for a devolved Northern Ireland Assembly with a power-sharing executive which was set up in 1999

immigrant a person who comes to live in a country they were not born in

inclusive ensuring that everyone is included, regardless of their background or material circumstances

interface areas an area where there is political tension or violence. In Northern Ireland it is where there is a Protestant/Unionist community living beside a Catholic/Nationalist community

Judicial system the system of courts within a particular country where the law of that country is applied and interpreted. The judicial system is usually part of the wider criminal justice system within a particular country

legal rights rights that everyone is entitled to by law

Ministers in Northern Ireland, elected members of the assembly who run government departments and come from different political parties

MLAs Members of the Legislative Assembly. There are 108 elected MLAs in the Northern Ireland Assembly

multicultural a society which is made up of a range of different cultural identities

Nationalist one of the two main cultural/political groups living in Northern Ireland. Most Nationalists are from the Catholic community and wish to be politically linked to the Republic of Ireland

NGOs Non-Governmental Organisations – charities, pressure groups and other voluntary and community groups which are not run by the government

peace process the name given to the period in Northern Ireland which covers the paramilitary ceasefires in 1994, the end of the worst of the 'Troubles', the Good Friday/Belfast Agreement 1998 (with the establishment of the Northern Ireland Assembly) and subsequent political developments

prejudice having inaccurate/irrational opinions about others and making judgements (pre-judging) about an individual or group without sound reason

pressure group NGOs and charities who put pressure on the government to change their policies and practice

referendum this is when registered voters are asked to express their opinion on an issue of public interest. In most referendums people vote to either accept or reject a particular proposal

relative poverty where people do not have adequate income or resources preventing them from enjoying a standard of living which would be regarded as acceptable by society generally

representation when you vote for a politician and they represent your views in the Northern Ireland Assembly – this is known as representation

sectarianism bigoted intolerance of other religious groups which can lead to prejudice, discrimination and violence between different religious groups

Section 75 this part of the Northern Ireland Act (1998) focuses on equality for minority groups. This Act not only made it illegal to discriminate, but also compulsory for government organisations and other public bodies to actively promote equality so that certain groups in society would have access to exactly the same opportunities as everyone else

sex discrimination discriminating against someone because of their gender

social inclusion ensuring that everyone is included in society. It also means making sure that no one is left out because of their material circumstances or because of the group that they belong to such as the homeless or unemployed

social responsibility having a concern for the welfare of others and behaving in such a way that ensures everyone is included in society

stereotyping having generalised views about a group and thinking that everyone in that group is the same, e.g. all football fans are hooligans

The Office of the First and Deputy First Ministers (OFMDFM) the government department who have responsibility for promoting a fair and inclusive society in Northern Ireland by supporting and overseeing the work of the other departments within the Northern Ireland Executive

UNICEF United Nations International Child Emergency Fund – this is an organisation which was set up by the United Nations to protect the rights of children around the world

Unionist one of the two main cultural/ political groups who live in Northern Ireland. Unionists are usually from the Protestant community and believe in maintaining strong cultural/political ties between Northern Ireland and Great Britain

United Nations Convention on the Rights of the Child (UNCRC) one of the most widely accepted documents on human rights in the world; it is a promise made by governments to protect the rights of all young people under the age of eighteen

Universal Declaration of Human Rights (UDHR) containing 30 Articles or 'promises', it is one of the most important documents on human rights in the world. Signed in 1948, it was written as a result of the atrocities of the Second World War. The countries who signed the document made a commitment to their citizens and to each other that they would promote and protect these human rights

voluntary groups groups who work within the community on a voluntary basis, without being paid

Glossary for Unit 2 Personal Development

absenteeism being late or not attending school or work

acquaintance someone you know but do not spend much time with

addiction a dependence on a substance: for example alcohol or drugs

anaemia a condition where the body has fewer red blood cells than it should and consequently oxygen does not get transported around the body effectively. This can lead to tiredness and fatigue

anorexia (nervosa) an eating disorder which occurs because a person has a distorted image of their body and which results in a loss or decline of appetite

bankruptcy a legal declaration that comes with certain restrictions when an individual is unable to pay their debts. As such their assets (money/houses/ car, etc.) are divided up equally among those who they owe money to

bereavement the death of an immediate family member or close friend

budget a document to predict or record income and expenses over a period of time

bulimia (nervosa) an eating disorder where a person eats a large amount of food in a short period of time (binge) then makes themselves sick to get rid of it

bullying bullying is a sustained form of abuse – whether it be verbal or physical, whereby one person or group usually intimidates a weaker person or group

calories on a food package label, a calorie refers to the amount of energy a serving of food has

central nervous system nerve endings send their signals to the brain and spinal cord which can lead to an involuntary reaction, for example the retraction of a hand when it touches a hot surface

Citizens Advice Bureau (CAB) charity providing free legal and financial advice to the public

Consumer Credit Counselling Service (CCCS) UK debt advice charity that offers free advice to help people become debt-free

credit the term used to describe obtaining goods or services without paying for them in full immediately but instead paying for them over an agreed term

creditor a person or group who is owed money

criminal justice system the system that deals with criminals, for example the courts

cyber bullying the act of bullying or intimidating another person using information technology; for example, a social networking site

cystic fibrosis a hereditary disease whereby an abnormal gene creates an abundance of mucus which makes it difficult to breathe and digest food

deficiency the absence of a nutrient in a person's body

dependency relying on something or someone

depression a mental state where a person's mood is low

depressants drugs that are used to slow down the central nervous system and brain activity

dieting changing eating habits to lose weight for health or cosmetic reasons

drugs any substance that affects how the body and mind work

dyscalculia a condition whereby a person finds maths concepts difficult

dyslexia a condition whereby a person finds it difficult to understand written words

eating disorder an abnormal or extreme eating habit, for example anorexia

euphoric a feeling of exhilaration and elation

eviction the process whereby a landlord legally removes a tenant from their property

exercise activity that can help improve health and should be part of a healthy lifestyle

expenditure a term used to describe the goods and services that money is spent on

haemophilia a genetic disorder which reduces the ability of blood clotting and as a result it can be difficult to stop bleeding

hallucinogens drugs that alter perceptions, moods and thoughts and can lead to users seeing things which do not exist

immune system this is the body's defence system which helps fight against disease

junk food the term used to describe food that is low in nutritional value and high in calories

lease a contract or an agreement between a tenant and a landlord

Glossary for Unit 2 Personal Development *continued*

loan agreement between a borrower and a lender to provide a sum of money upfront that is to be repaid later

maternity leave term generally used to describe a woman's extended leave of absence from work during pregnancy and when their child has been born. Maternity leave arrangements vary between employers but normally allow women to stay off work for several months and they are usually paid during this period

media various forms of communication; for example TV, radio, newspapers and magazines

morals and values beliefs that are usually inherited or instilled in us by our parents

mortgage a mortgage is a term used to describe a loan that is used to purchase a house or other property. Generally the mortgage is secured against the property and is paid off over a long period of time

needs something that is essential for survival such as food, water, clothing, shelter and heat

negative equity a term used to describe an asset that is worth less than a loan used to buy it. This term is often used when a mortgage taken out to buy a house is higher than the current value of the house. An example of this would be taking out a mortgage for £150,000 and then selling the house for £125,000 as this would mean owing £25,000 for a house you no longer own

net income money left over after total expenditure is subtracted from total income. If the result is negative then the expenditure is more than the money coming in

NHS National Health Service – free, government-run health care provider in the UK

Northern Ireland Community Addiction Service (NICAS) charity that can help with drug/alcohol addiction

obesity the term used to describe excess body fat as calculated using the Body Mass Index (BMI)

opiates the term used to describe drugs produced from opium found in the poppy plant

organic refers to foods that have been grown naturally without synthetic fertilisers or pesticides

osteoporosis a disease that makes bones less dense, more fragile and prone to fracturing

paternity leave This is similar to maternity leave but most often refers to the leave taken by a new born baby's father. Unlike maternity leave, paternity leave allows a father to take several weeks of paid leave rather than several months

peer pressure the influence that a friend or a 'peer' can have on you

pen pal someone you correspond with via letter

profit profit is a term used in business to describe the amount of money earned after all associated expenses are subtracted. For example, if you buy a car for £1000 and then sell it on for £1200 you will have made £200 profit

property ladder this is a phrase used to define a person's gradual climb from owning a cheaper property to a more expensive property. 'Getting on the property ladder' would mean buying a house for the first time

rehabilitation method used to help overcome issues such as drug/alcohol addiction that usually involves withdrawing from society and living on site for a period of time

relapse this occurs when a person is re-affected by something they have been affected by in the past, for example a drug addiction

rental agreement document that sets out the terms and conditions between a landlord and tenant – for example, how much rent is to be paid by the tenant to the landlord is agreed

self-esteem how you see/feel about yourself

self harm deliberate harming of oneself, for example cutting, scratching or pulling out hair

siblings brothers or sisters

SMART targets method of setting targets to help achieve goals – stands for Specific, Measurable, Achievable, Realistic, Time bound

social development process by which a person develops the social skills necessary to function in society

social networking the term used to describe interaction with others using the Internet

social stigma belief that others look down on certain individuals or groups of people

stimulant a drug that can be used to increase alertness or improve physical performance

stroke a medical condition where oxygen to the brain is temporarily lost

suicide the act of taking your own life; killing yourself

tenant a person who pays rent on a property they live in

targets series of smaller steps required to reach a goal

trust faith or confidence in another person or thing to do what is expected or required

wants things that are not necessary but make life more enjoyable

WHO World Health Organisation – a United Nations body that monitors health trends and provides leadership on global health issues

withdrawal symptoms unpleasant effects the body may experience when it no longer receives something it relies upon

Glossary for Unit 3 Employability

Competency a skill that an individual is good at doing

Contract of employment a document which contains terms and conditions of employment

Design a term used to describe how a business goes about inventing and making a product or service

Emigration the movement of people to another country

Employment when someone is paid to work for a company or organisation

Employment patterns the types of jobs people are employed in at a certain point in time

Entrepreneur a person who has taken a risk in order to carry out a business venture (usually to start up a business)

Exports goods or services that are sold to another country

Global economy the international exchange of money, goods and ideas across countries' geographical boundaries

Global economic changes changes and fluctuations in the economy caused by events that happen throughout the world

Globalisation the movement of goods, people, and ideas around the world

Immigration the process of coming to live in a foreign country

Imports goods or services which are brought into a country from another country

Induction the process of introducing a new employee to the workings of a business. It will usually include information about health and safety and an understanding of the business' history and goals

Interview technique behaviour and characteristics that should be displayed at interviews

Job shadowing when a new employee follows, watches and learns from an established employee in a particular job role so that he/she can understand what the job involves and the skills required

Lifelong learning the process of continuing to develop skills, knowledge and expertise throughout life

Market This is the term used to describe how a business goes about promoting and selling a product or service

Migration the process of people moving between countries

New technologies new advancements, ideas, methods or inventions in the field of technology

Off the job training training that is conducted outside the workplace

On the job training training that is conducted within the workplace

Qualities personality traits of an individual

Recruitment the process of applying for work

Redundant when a person's job is no longer required by the business because of changes in working practices or financial cuts

Self-employment when a person works for his/herself – he/she is their own boss

Skills abilities that an individual may have to offer

Training learning a new skill or piece of knowledge, usually in order to perform a job or to improve current working practices

Index